SMOOTHIE COOKBOOK

Simple Guide to Learn How to Include and Use Superfoods

(Best Protein Smoothies, Easy to Make Weight Loss Smoothies)

John Clark

Published by Sharon Lohan

© **John Clark**

All Rights Reserved

Smoothie Cookbook: Simple Guide to Learn How to Include and Use Superfoods (Best Protein Smoothies, Easy to Make Weight Loss Smoothies)

ISBN 978-1-990334-42-9

All rights reserved. No part of this guide may be reproduced in any form without permission in writing from the publisher except in the case of brief quotations embodied in critical articles or reviews.

Legal & Disclaimer

The information contained in this book is not designed to replace or take the place of any form of medicine or professional medical advice. The information in this book has been provided for educational and entertainment purposes only.

The information contained in this book has been compiled from sources deemed reliable, and it is accurate to the best of the Author's knowledge; however, the Author cannot guarantee its accuracy and validity and cannot be held liable for any errors or omissions. Changes are periodically made to this book. You must consult your doctor or get professional medical advice before using any of the suggested remedies, techniques, or information in this book.

Table of contents

Part 1 1
Introduction 2
Chapter 1: Getting Started On Smoothies 3
Chapter 2: The Process Of Fat Burning 7
Chapter 3: Super Foods That Do You Good 10
Chapter 4: A Sample Of Some Of The Best Recipes For A Healthy Body 14
Chapter 5: Best Workouts For Every Level Of Fitness 16
Chapter 6: The 21 Day Challenge 19
Conclusion 27
Part 2 28
Energy Smoothies 29
Supreme Smoothie 30
Mango And Peach Smoothie 31
Cocoa and Peanut Butter Smoothie 32
Coffee Smoothie 33
Super Food Smoothie 34
Berry Smoothie 34
Beetroot Smoothie 35
Orange And Flax Seed Smoothie 36
Banana Nuts And Cocoa Smoothie 37
Avocado And Coconut Smoothie 38
Memory Booster Smoothies 39
Berry Medley 39

- Dates And Walnuts Smoothie 40
- Cantaloupe And Raw Egg Smoothie 41
- Cleanse Smoothies 42
- Go Green Smoothie 42
- Green Smoothie 43
- Best Cleanse Smoothie 44
- Kale Smoothie 45
- Detoxifying Smoothie 46
- Low Sugar/Diabetic Smoothies 47
- Low Carb Green Smoothie 48
- Diabetic Oatmeal Smoothie 49
- Pineapple And Spinach Smoothie 50
- Peach Smoothie For Dietetics 51
- Dessert Smoothies 52
- Apple Dessert Smoothie 52
- Caramel Smoothie 53
- Key Lime Yoplait Smoothie Recipe 54
- Peanut Butter Smoothie 55
- Oreo Smoothie 56
- Dairy Free Smoothies 57
- Sunshine Smoothie 57
- Granny Smith Apples Smoothie 58
- Banana And Nuts Smoothie 59
- Pineapple And Avocado Smoothie 60
- Soymilk Smoothie 61
- Cocoa And Macadamia Smoothie 62
- Ketogenic Smoothies 63

Peanut Butter Caramel Milkshake	63
Blueberry Smoothie	64
Blackberry Chocolate Smoothie	65
Cherry Vanilla Smoothie	66
Keto Strawberry Milkshake	67
High Protein Smoothie	68
Pomegranate And Beetroot Smoothie	68
Raspberry Almond Chia Smoothie	69
Peanut Butter And Jelly Smoothie	70
Green Banana Smoothie	71
Very Berry Smoothie	72
Smoothies For Gout & Arthritis	73
Smoothie To Help With Gout	73
Kiwi And Kale Smoothie	74
Melon-Mango Smoothie	75
Strawberry-Orange Smoothie	76
Grapefruit Smoothie	77
Best Smoothies By Blood Type	78
Smoothie For Type A Blood Type	78
Smoothie For Type B Blood Type	79
Smoothie For Type Ab Blood Type	80
Smoothie For Type O Blood Type	81
Berry Coconut Smoothie	82
Island Dream Smoothie	83
Smoothie A La Orange	84
Creamy Lime Chiller	85
Summer's Bliss Smoothie	86

- Java Chiller Smoothie 87
- Chunky Monkey Smoothie 88
- Pineapple Mango Smoothie 89
- Cookies And Cream Smoothie 90
- Carrot Smoothie 91
- Green Mango Shake 92
- Cocoa Cream Smoothie 93
- Strawberry Smoothie 94
- Mixed Fruit Shake 95
- Clean Breeze Smoothie 96
- Sunburst Smoothie 97
- Avocado Smoothie 98
- Classic Fruit And Yogurt Smoothie 99
- Peaches N Cream Smoothie 100
- Strawberry Banana Smoothie 101
- 1.1 Morning Glory Smoothie 102
- 1.2 Wake Me Up Smoothie! 103
- 1.3 Pomegranate-Banana Oats Morning Smoothie 104
- 1.4 Avocado and Agave nectar smoothie 105
- 1.5 Banana and Yogurt-Granola Smoothie 106
- 1.6 Supercharge Morning Smoothie 107
- 1.7 Peaches and Coconut Smoothie 108
- 1.8 Minty Mango- Soy Milk Smoothie 109
- 1.9 Raspberry-Pistachio and Goji Berry -Oats Smoothie 110
- 1.10 Blueberry Almond-Muesli Smoothie 111
- 2.1 Pomegranate and Wild Mulberry Smoothie 112
- 2.2 Spinach and Mixed berry Smoothie 113

2.3 Beetroot, Apple-Blackberry Smoothie 114

2.4 Kiwi- Pineapple Green Tea Smoothie 115

2.5 Cucumber, Red bell Pepper and Pear Smoothie 116

2.6 Avocado and Banana Smoothie 117

2.7 Beetroot and Watermelon Smoothie 118

2.8 Carrot, Tomato and Apple Smoothie 119

2.9 The Orange Delight 120

2.10 The Green Monster 121

3.1 Citrusy Spinach and Mango Delight 122

3.2 The Anti oxidant Surprise 123

3.3 Beautiful Complexion Smoothie 124

3.4 The Vitamin C Surprise 125

3.5 The Sunny Smoothie 126

3.6 Blueberry and Passion Fruit Oats Smoothie 127

3.7 Dragon Fruit and Swiss-Chard almond Smoothie 128

3.8 Fabulous Skin Smoothie 129

3.9 Pink in your cheeks Smoothie 130

3.10 Mixed Berry, Spinach and Orange smoothie 131

4.1 Cucumber and Coconut Smoothie 132

4.2 Spicy Watermelon and Cantaloupe Smoothie 133

4.3 Strawberry, Spinach and Lemonade Smoothie 134

4.4 Spinach, Green Apple and Cucumber Smoothie 135

4.5 Yoghurt and Papaya smoothie 136

4.6 Cucumber, Raspberry and Pineapple Smoothie 137

4.7 Blueberry, Watermelon and Tomato Medley 138

4.8 Summer Bonanza! 139

4.9 Strawberry-Grape and Coconut water Smoothie 140

4.10 Iceberg Lettuce, Star Fruit and Pear Smoothie 141
5.1 Watermelon, Beetroot and Date Smoothie 142
5.2 Spinach, Kiwi and Hemp Smoothie 143
5.3 Dragon Fruit, Spinach and Blueberry Smoothie 144
5.4 Mango, Apricot and Kale Smoothie 145
5.5 Figs, Spinach and Strawberry Smoothie 146
5.6 Kale, Honey Dew and Date Smoothie 147
5.7 Avocado, Collard Greens and Figs Smoothie 148
5.8 Blueberry, Orange and Vanilla Yoghurt Smoothie 149
5.9 Pineapple, Strawberry and Grape Fruit Smoothie 150
5.10 Dragon Fruit, Carrot and Kale Smoothie with Cocoa ... 151
6.1 Mango Vanilla Smoothie 152
6.2 Blueberry and Coconut Surprise 153
6.3. Vanilla Yoghurt and Raspberry Smoothie 154
6.4 Omega 3 Rich Peach Smoothie 155
6.5 Apple and Coconut-Vanilla Smoothie 156
6.6 Pineapple and Spiced Pumpkin Smoothie 157
6.7 Strawberry and Pomegranate Smoothie 158
6.8 Green Tea, Kale and Papaya Smoothie 159
6.9 The Green Delight Smoothie 160
6.10 Papaya, Banana and Green apple Smoothie 161
7.1 Honeydew, Cucumber and Ginger Smoothie 162
7.2 Apple, Apple Cider Vinegar and Beetroot Smoothie 163
7.3 Banana, Avocado and Aloe Vera Smoothie 163
7.4 Green Tea, Papaya and Spinach Smoothie 164
7.5 Pineapple, Avocado and Parsley Smoothie 165
7.6 Super Smoothie with garlic and ACV 165

7.7 Kale, Almond Milk and Mixed Berry Smoothie 166
7.8 Mango and Papaya Smoothie with Turmeric................. 167
7.9 Cranberry and Creamy Coconut Smoothie 167
7.10 Dragon Fruit-Avocado and Almond Milk Smoothie....... 168
8.1 Creamy Avocado and Cucumber Smoothie...................... 169
8.2 Peach, Spinach and Banana Smoothie............................. 170
8.3 Pineapple, Spinach and Almond Milk Smoothie................ 170
4. Kale, Banana and Spirulina Smoothie 171
8.5 Dandelion, Apple and Flaxseed Smoothie 172
8.6 Carrot, Avocado and Ginger Smoothie................................ 173
8.7 Romaine Lettuce, Pineapple and Pumpkin Seed Smoothie
.... 173
8.8 Minty Kale, Strawberry-Coconut Smoothie......................... 174
8.9 Avocado, Baby Greens and Date Smoothie 175
8.10 Kale, Grapes and Cucumber Smoothie 175
9.1 Pineapple and Ginger Smoothie.. 176
9.2 Sweet and Creamy Spinach Smoothie............................... 177
9.3 Papaya, Pineapple and Carrot Smoothie.......................... 178
9.4 Pumpkin, Pear and Ginger Smoothie................................. 178
9.5 Kale, Yoghurt and Banana Smoothie................................ 179
9.6 Beetroot, Cucumber and Green Apple Smoothie 180
9.7 Broccoli, Strawberry and Almond Milk Smoothie............ 180
9.8 Avocado, Spinach and Green Grapes Smoothie 181
9.9 Carrot, Beetroot and Apple Smoothie 182
10. Kale and Grapefruit Smoothie.. 183
10.1 Raspberry - Pomegranate Smoothie 183
10.2 Almond and Mixed Berry smoothie.................................. 184

10.3 Banana and Apple-Ginger Smoothie 185

10.4 Green tea, Berry and Papaya Smoothie 186

10.5 Pineapple and Pistachio Yoghurt Smoothie 186

10.6 Spinach, Kiwi and Pear Smoothie 187

10.7 Tropical Blast Smoothie. **Error! Bookmark not defined.**

10.8 Peach and Apricot Smoothie**Error! Bookmark not defined.**

10.9 Banana- Cashew Soy Smoothie**Error! Bookmark not defined.**

10.10 Mango, Hazelnut and Bee Pollen Smoothie............... **Error! Bookmark not defined.**

Part 1

Introduction

The tasty concoctions in this book can contain peanut butter, succulent fruits and even a bit of dark chocolate and still be within your daily calorie limit. You are really not losing out on your favorite food when you go on this 21 day plan for weight loss and good health. You will come out of this experience slimmer and healthier than ever.

If you are ready to start losing weight flip on to the next page to find out what a smoothie is and what it can do for you.

Chapter 1: Getting Started On Smoothies

Smoothies are a fun way to lose weight. They are easy to make and require very little prep time on your end. All of the ingredients you will need to make them are also readily available in supermarkets and groceries. They help satisfy hunger and provide you with the nutrients that you need to go about your daily tasks. They are tasty and easy to incorporate into any kind of diet.

The calories that your smoothie will contain will be dictated by you as you control the amount of fruit or vegetable you add to it. When you control the calories, you control how much your body is taking in. The right amount of calories from these smoothies together with a healthy diet and some exercise can help you lose weight in the best possible way.

This book contains tips on how to make healthy smoothies that also taste great. It contains ideas for what kinds of smoothies to make for breakfast, lunch, and dinner. You will not run out of tasty ideas when you use this book to guide you in mixing up your healthy smoothies.

As an added bonus and to help you truly achieve the weight you want, you will also get some great weight loss tips, exercise tips, and nutrition facts about your favorite smoothie. You will get the best recipes that are easy to make for when you are on the go and the best ones to make when you have a little more time on your hands. If you need to run a marathon, for example, there's a smoothie to help you with endurance and keeping up your strength. If you need to become stronger to be able to compete for a weight lifting contest, there's also an easy smoothie recipe for that.

What are Smoothies?

The origin of the smoothie is unknown. It is a well-known food processing technique that people all over the world are familiar with. No matter where you go smoothies, can be found. No single person owns the right to a certain smoothie like a patent or anything like that. But some nutrition and fitness experts create their own secret blend of smoothies to market as their own.

Smoothies are made by combining or blending fruits, vegetable, and other food products such as milk and ice. These are placed in a blender to crush, mix, and smooth them together until the mixture becomes slush - thus, the name smoothie.

People all over the world have used smoothies countless number of times to help them with weight loss. That's because smoothies with the right ingredients provide nutrients for the body without all the added calories. Smoothies can be nutritious, delicious, and still help you lose weight.

When creating smoothies, people also tend to add ingredients that provide some texture such as oats and nuts. Others like to make smoothies that are creamy by adding a cup or two of yogurt or milk. When ice cream is added to fruits, it becomes more like a milk shake instead of a smoothie.

Smoothie flavors are limited only by your imagination. In order for a smoothie to help in weight loss, it must contain more vegetables and fruits and less sugar and other sweet ingredients. For some, this can make the taste of the smoothie a bit bitter. There are some, however, that prefer drinking the same ingredients in a smoothie instead of eating the actual vegetables such as kale, spinach and other dark green leafy vegetables.

Smoothies also add variety in taste to weight loss diets. Most weight loss diets seem monotonous with all the leafy greens that one has to eat daily. People can get bored eating the same thing. They may also feel deprived because they cannot eat their favorite food. Adding a smoothie made from naturally sweet fruits such as raspberries and blueberries into the mix may help make eating these boring old greens palatable because of their sweeter, fruitier taste.

Some people, especially when they are on a special weight loss program, tend to miss out on important nutrients from food because they are consuming less of it. One of the most common nutrients that dieters avoid like crazy is carbohydrates. Carbohydrates, or carbs as they are often referred to, provide you with energy to power you through the day. They come from starchy food such as rice and wheat. When people are in some weight loss programs, carbs are often minimized and sometimes eliminated from the diet. Smoothies are great sources of missing nutrients when powder supplements and herbal supplements are added.

Smoothies are great because they provide the body with added fiber that the body needs. Some people do not get enough fiber in their body making it difficult for them to lose weight. The fiber in blended fruits and vegetables increases your fiber intake easily. Fiber makes smoothies healthful so people add a huge dose of vegetables into smoothies. Compared to fruit juices, smoothies are often considered better because of their dietary fiber content.

From this chapter, you have learned how big the role of smoothie is in weight loss and maintaining a healthy weight. The next chapter will talk about fat burning and smoothies that can help in this area.

Chapter 2: The Process Of Fat Burning

Fat burning is the process of eliminating excess fat in the body. To effectively do this, a person should exercise and increase his metabolism. This phase of losing weight is very hard especially for people who have accumulated a lot of fats in their body. Some people have to work out doubly just to remove an ounce of fat. And even then, it may not be enough.

People have to go through special diets with lesser calorie count to lose stubborn fat. This can leave a person feeling tired because of the lack of energy and nutrients. In order to strike a balance, people going through the weight loss process can add smoothies into their diet. These drinks can help deliver the right amount of nutrients with less calories.

It has been repeated many times that smoothies aid in the fat burning process. Here's how they work in detail:

1.Fat burning supplements can be easily added to smoothies – there is no need to mix other kinds of juices and drinks in order to add fat burning supplements to your diet. You can just pour whatever supplements you need to take into the mix of smoothie ingredients and you can drink them all in one go. Fat burning supplements also often do not taste that good. When added to fruit smoothies, they become more palatable.

2.Smoothies can be make eating fat burning ingredients easier – if you are not a fan of eating grapefruit, kale, and other dark leafy vegetables, putting all of them in smoothie form may help you digest them easily. When mixed with other fruits such as lemons, berries, and similar tastier fruits, the unpleasant taste of the food you dislike will not be as offensive to your taste buds anymore. You can hardly taste these food when mixed with better tasting ingredients.

3.Smoothies can make use of ingredients that are not commonly food in most recipes – again, mixing up smoothie ingredients depend on you and the flavors you prefer. You can add ingredients that are difficult to eat on their own or to incorporate into food recipes. Whey, for example, is not commonly found in most recipes. You can add whey powder into your smoothie recipe to enjoy the ingredient's fat burning benefits.

4.Smoothies make you feel fuller longer – some smoothies are full of dietary fiber that makes you feel fuller longer. When you are constantly full, you tend to consume less food. When the body consumes less food, it burns stored fat in order to provide your body with the energy it needs. This results to easier and effective weight loss for you.

5.Smoothies may help boost metabolism – as people age, their metabolism becomes slower. This is the reason why you seem to have the appetite of a gorilla when you were a teenage, but never got fat. When you became an adult, everything you eat seems to add to your weight. Drinking smoothies with metabolism enhancing ingredients will help speed up your metabolism and burn fat faster.

Smoothies are delicious ways to make your body burn fat faster. The next chapter will talk about super foods that can aid in weight loss.

Chapter 3: Super Foods That Do You Good

In the world of weight loss and diets, there are certain foods that should be a staple on your grocery shopping list. These are called super foods. Super foods not only stimulate weight loss but also provide the body with nutrients that it needs.

Super foods are called as such because they provide the body with more nutrients, vitamins, and minerals than most other food. They provide the body with more benefits that no other food can. Some of these super foods are found in the list below:

1.Oats – oats add fiber to a person's diet. As you know, fiber makes you feel full longer so adding them to your smoothie may help you lose weight. The fiber in oats also aid in proper digestion and makes it easy for you to regulate your bowels.

2.Tuna – rich in omega three fatty acids, tuna is a low calorie food that has a high protein content. It is a popular choice for body builders who want to keep their protein intake high but would not like to add more calories into their diet.

3.Whole eggs – eggs were once feared for their high cholesterol content. It turns out that people were just misinformed and that eggs are safe for daily consumption. They are high in protein that can help you feel full for longer. When added to regular meals, eggs may provide you with lesser calories if you are going through a strict diet.

4.Green leafy vegetables – a healthy and balanced diet is never complete without a huge dose of green leafy vegetables. These types of food provide fiber, minerals and other nutrients that may aid in making you lose weight. They are more filling than most sugary food so you do not feel hungry easily. Kale and spinach are some great examples of green leafy vegetables that you should be adding to your diet. These two vegetables are also common ingredients in many healthy smoothie mixes.

5.Lean meat – lean meat contains more protein and less fat. Lean meat may include lean beef and white meat in chicken. Lean meat has less calorie content and less cholesterol content than meats high in fat.

6.Tomatoes – tomatoes contain lycopene which is not commonly found in many foods. Lycopene is a known antioxidant that can help fight certain cancers. Many studies suggest that getting a good dose of lycopene found in tomatoes can help lower cholesterol and help prevent some cancers. Tomatoes are also high vitamin C, fiber, and potassium.

7.Beans – beans contain fiber, protein, and minerals without the added fat content. They can add antioxidants and energy boosting iron that can help your power through the day. Burritos and stews are some great examples of bean dishes you can try.

8. Garlic – known as vampire repellants, garlic is a great source of nutrients that can help lower blood pressure and reduce cholesterol. Though garlic may not be a great tasting ingredient in making smoothies, it's a great food to have at home. Add it to your dishes to increase your super food intake.

9. Cruciferous vegetables – an example of this kind of vegetable is broccoli. They contain nutrients called phytonutrients that can help suppress the growth of certain tumors. This also helps reduce the risk of you getting cancer. Foods in this category are also rich in vitamin C which helps boost your immune system and folic acid.

10. Apples – there is some truth to the saying an apple a day keeps the doctor away. These sweet fruits contain high levels of antioxidants that help fight cancer. They are also great alternatives to coffee and can help wake you up during those afternoon slumps.

11. Avocado – this guacamole staple is rich in vitamin E and healthy fat that keeps you feeling satisfied longer. These also taste great in smoothies.

12. Olives – olives provide heart healthy fats so that you can cook your favorite food minus all the unwanted artery clogging fats. They make great additions to pasta dishes as well as salad dressings.

13. Brown rice – brown rice contains loads of fiber to aid in better digestion. This also helps you feel fuller so

you do not consume more. It is one of the best sources for magnesium.

14. Oysters – oysters contain selenium and zinc. Zinc helps boost your immune system and protects you from becoming sick.

15. Berries – fruits such as raspberries and blackberries are rich in phytochemicals that may reduce the growth of certain cancers. Fruits are naturally sweet so you do not need to add sugar to any fruit smoothie. Fruits are also rich in fiber especially if you add the skin when blending your smoothies.

These are just some of the super foods you need to have in your home. There are so much more food that are considered super foods. Learn more about these foods and try to incorporate them into your daily diet. The next chapter will learn more about the best recipes for these super foods and other types of food.

Chapter 4: A Sample Of Some Of The Best Recipes For A Healthy Body

If all that talk of super foods has not gotten you hungry yet, this section will truly have you salivating. Here you will find some of the best super food recipes for food and smoothies that you can include in your diet for weight loss:

Breakfast

1. Pumpkin Spiced Oatmeal –to make this delicious and filling breakfast, cook 1 cup of oats following the cooking instructions on the pack. Use 2 cups of 1.5% milk as your cooking liquid. Once the oatmeal is cooked, mix in half a cup of pumpkin puree. Add 2 tablespoons of agave or honey and one fourth teaspoon each of ground cinnamon and nutmeg. Serve warm.

Salad

2. Balsamic Cucumber Salad – Combine the following ingredients in a large bowl: 1 large cucumber, sliced and halved; 2 cups of cherry tomatoes, also halved; and 1 medium red onion that's been thinly sliced. Pour in half a cup of balsamic vinaigrette slowly as you toss your ingredients. Top the salad with 3/4 cup of crumbled feta cheese.

Small Meal

2. Shrimp Tacos and Black Bean and Mango Salsa

In a medium sized bowl, toss together rinsed black beans (contents of a 15 oz. can), a large ripe mango, one seeded jalapeno, 2 tablespoon of fresh lime juice, and one fourth teaspoon of salt and pepper. Fold in half cup of cilantro.

Next, season 24 medium sized shrimps with 1/4 tsp. of both cayenne pepper and salt. Cook shrimp in a large skillet on high heat, turning it once until it becomes opaque. Fill soft tortillas with the shrimp and beans and mango salsa and serve with lime wedges.

Smoothies

3. Kale, Almond, and Banana Smoothie with Chia Seeds – mix the following ingredients in a blender until smooth: 1 1/2 cups kale, packed in; 1 cup almond or rice milk; 1 tbsp. almond butter; 1 tbsp. chia seeds; 1 tbsp. coconut oil; and 1/2 of a ripe banana. Drink immediately.

4. Banana Ginger Smoothie– combine 1 sliced banana with ¾ cup of vanilla yogurt, 1 tbsp. of honey, and ½ tsp. freshly grated ginger in a blender until smooth. This healthy breakfast smoothie can help soothe digestion and other stomach problems.

Chapter 5: Best Workouts For Every Level Of Fitness

The best kinds of workouts are the ones that do not require an expensive gym membership, can be done anywhere, and can be completed in no time. If you think this sounds impossible, think again. With commitment and determination, you can actually have the best workouts that give you the results that you are working so hard for.

Here are some of the best workouts you can do at home or anywhere else. They do not cost much and can be done at your own pace:

Yoga

Yoga is one of the best forms of exercise. It promotes relaxation and meditation. Whether you are a beginner who does not want something too strenuous or a very athletic person who wants to challenge yourself, yoga has something for you. It has breathing exercises and poses that promote weight loss and other health benefits for the mind and body. It is fairly inexpensive as you will only need a yoga mat and a routine that you can follow. You can find a number of routines programmed for various fitness goals online. Do yoga with friends and family to make it more fun.

Pilates

The beefed up sister of yoga is Pilates. This type of exercise involves a lot of stretching and testing your body's limits. It aims to make you more flexible, lean, and adaptable. There are several places that are not gyms that offer Pilates classes. You simply need to find one that has classes or sessions that fit your schedule and lifestyle the most.

Strength Training

Strength training is a great way to lose weight. When you do this kind of exercise, you are increasing muscle mass and burning fat at the same time. The more muscles versus fat you have, the faster your metabolism is. Lean muscle burns fat more efficiently.

Cardio

Get your running shoes on and start some a great cardio routine. For some people cardio is the first step towards weight loss. It is easy to do and can be done just about anywhere. You can go running, jogging, or swimming. You can also join a kickboxing class and other fitness classes. Classes in ballet, jazz, pole dancing, belly dancing, and Zumba are different dance forms that give you fun cardio activities to try.

Play Any Kind of Sports

Join a local softball team and incorporate fun into your workout. Play a few rounds of tennis every week with your best friend and see who can beat whom. Make workouts fun by doing different kinds of sports that allow you to work up a sweat.

Some of the best kinds of sports activities you can try are soccer, basketball, volleyball, and baseball. Joining sports teams also builds your network and group of friends. You get a good workout and gain new experiences at the same time. That's two birds in one stone.

Mountain Climbing

Not for the faint of heart, mountain climbing, and hiking are some of the best forms of exercise because of the unpredictable terrains that you will encounter. In regular workouts, you will have to follow a routine. Over time, your body becomes accustomed to the routine and you do not burn as much calories as before. Mountain climbing, on the other hand, allows you to have a different exercise with every different mountain that you climb. If you cannot go on hikes due to bad weather, you can still try indoor wall climbing.

Surfing

Not to be confused with going through different websites on the internet, water surfing is a great workout that you can do if you live anywhere near the ocean. Surfing exercises your legs, arms, and entire body as you fluidly glide through the different waves. As bonus points, you get that healthy tan after a surf in the ocean.

Chapter 6: The 21 Day Challenge

Now that you know what the different ways to lose weight are, it's time to apply it to your life in a 21 day challenge. This 21 day challenge is not something that you should treat lightly. It entails commitment and dedication in order for you to succeed.

Before you begin this challenge, it is important that you have yourself checked by a doctor to see if you are fit enough to complete this challenge. Some of these challenges will test your willpower and others will test your strength. You must check with the doctor to see how much your body can take and what precautions you have to take.

Once you have mentally and physically prepared for the challenge, you may start the 21 day challenge any time. Try to start it on days when you have no pending travel or have a big event happening in your life so you can focus solely on the challenge.

Day 1 – Chuck the bad foods

Remove all refined, processed food from your home. This purging process helps keep temptation away. Take away food that are high in sugar and high in fats and donate them to a local feeding shelter.

Day 2 – Plan your food for the next weeks

Draw up a plan on what you are going to eat for the week and the following week. Choose food products that are low in calorie but pack a lot of energy into every bite. Find a variety of food and smoothie mixes as shown in the previous chapters. Plan your menus for breakfast, lunch, dinner, and snacks.

Day 3 - Buy good food

With your fridge nearly empty, you should start filling it up with some of the super foods listed in the earlier chapters. Aim to buy food products that are rich in fiber and fat burning ingredients. Buy food from local markets and make sure that they are fresh. Do not fall into 100 calorie food traps. These are laden with extenders and artificial flavor to make them palatable. They are also often full of sugars. Stick to the fresh produce section of the grocery whenever you buy food.

Buy food with ingredients that you can pronounce. Foods with less than 5 ingredients are also great because you are not using as much calorie filled ingredients. Check the label for important nutrients.

Day 4 – Start with some light cardio

It's time to start exercising if you really want to jumpstart your weight loss. A light cardio may come in the form of jogging, brisk walking or aerobic exercise. Do it for at least 30 minutes. After this time, you should feel tired but not to the point that you are about to pass out.

If you feel like you cannot complete the 30 minutes, it is alright to stop and rest. Do not force yourself to do something that will cause injury to your body. You have just started this challenge so it is natural to want to rest for a few minutes as your body is not accustomed yet to the new physical activities you are adding to your daily routine.

Day 5 – Keep moving

Move frequently throughout the day to increase your chances of losing weight. Instead of sending an email to a colleague who sits a few rows ahead of you, why not walk up to him and talk to him face to face. Walking and standing up are great ways to get you up and off your butt in the office.

You can also try getting off one stop before your actual bus stop and walk the rest of the way to add some light exercise. This small change can mean more calories burned per day.

Day 6 – Stop drinking high calorie drinks

Today, you start saying no to soda and sugary drinks. If you are craving for a tasty drink, do not reach for a soda. These are filled with sugar and unwanted calories. Go for a smoothie instead. A good berry mix energizes your day and gives you so much fiber that soda does not have. It is also very filling so you won't feel too hungry during the day.

Day 7 – Replace one meal with a smoothie

A good smoothie such as a peanut butter and banana smoothie can provide you with proteins and energy that you need for the day. Replace one of your meals with just a smoothie and see how it works for you. If you feel you cannot replace one meal, try to drink a smoothie with a smaller meal instead.

Day 8 – See how you are doing with the food choices in your meal plan

Today is the time to evaluate your meal plan and identify your success and fail points. See which food items in your meal plan were able to sustain you through the day. Keep them in your meal plan for the next weeks and find similar food that you can add to your list.

Identify food items that you found difficult to stick to or that you did not really enjoy that much. Scratch them out from your meal plan and replace them with those that you are more likely to stick to.

Day 9 – Go for more frequent but smaller meals in a day

Smaller meals throughout the day keep your energy levels up and fill you up better than taking in three big meals a day. Revisit your meal plan and tweak the items on your list accordingly. Make one of your small meals an all- vegetable smoothie to increase your vegetable intake.

Day 10 – Level up your exercise

By this time, your 30 minute exercise should already have become a regular routine. Your body has gotten used to the exercises so you need to change them up. Add some weight training to your daily exercise routine. You do not have to lift incredibly heavy weights all at once. Start with 3-5 pounds and do more sets and reps instead of using heavier weights.

Day 11 – Increase your water intake

Water is calorie free and is inexpensive. Adding more water to your diet helps you remove the toxins from your body. It keeps you from becoming dehydrated and thirsty. Sometimes, you do not really feel hungry. You mistake your body's cues as hunger rather than thirst. If you feel this way, try drinking a glass of water first. If after 10 minutes you still feel hungry, go ahead and eat.

Day 12 – Add more fiber to your diet

Fiber helps keep you feeling full longer. Add a good smoothie filled with oats, berries, and apples for an energizing drink. Smoothies with these ingredients contain high levels of fiber to help you curb your hunger.

Day 13 – Add all natural spices to your food

Do not reach for the salt immediately to add flavor to your food. Reach for different spices instead. Use cinnamon, rosemary, or oregano to add flavor and depth to regular food. Experiment with different kinds of spices and see what works for your palate the best.

Day 14 – Check your progress

Do not be afraid of stepping on the weighing scale. You will want to know how far you have come after almost two weeks into the 21 day challenge. It will give you motivation to see that you have lost weight and fuel your drive to lose more. Tracking your progress also helps you know how much more work you need to do in order to achieve your dream weight.

Day 15 – Snack on low calorie food

Keep dried nuts and fruits in your food stash instead of those calorie filled chips and other sugary snacks. Almonds, dried dates and other fiber rich snacks can give keep your hunger at bay and are low in calories. These should be your go-to snacks from this day forward.

Day 16 – Add some spice to your life

Spicy food can help curb hunger. Capsaicin which is regularly found in chili triggers the release of endorphins in your brain. Endorphins make you feel happy. When you are happy and satisfied, you can't think of being hungry.

Day 17 – Add bigger portions of green leafy vegetables

Instead of filling your plate with carbs such as pasta and mashed potatoes, provide a bigger space for salads and other dark green vegetables. You can do a ratio of half a plate of greens, a quarter plate of proteins, and a quarter plate of carbs.

Day 18 – Trim the fat off

Go fat free today. Choose lean meats such as turkey and white meat from chicken breasts. Remove the skin and just eat the meat. For beef and pork, trim the fat and grill instead of frying. Stop frying food altogether. Oils used in frying add unwanted fat and calories to your food.

Day 19 – Use smaller plates and sit down when you eat

Smaller plates give the illusion of having a fuller plate. You are tricking your mind into thinking that you have more food than you actually do. Do not eat on the go. Savor your food in a sit down meal. Talk with friends and do not wolf down the food on your plate in successive mouthfuls.

Day 20 – Add soup to your diet

Soups are filling and contain less calories than a full meal. Try a healthy tomato soup. You can also try making a tomato smoothie with some carrots, lemon juice, and ice.

Day 21 – Take deep breaths

Start incorporating deep breathing exercises into your routine. Whenever you find yourself feeling hungry, try to breathe deeply for a few minutes. Deep breathing slows down your heart rate making you feel relaxed and reducing your stress hormones.

Try to take a walk in a park to see if you can curb your hunger. If after a walk in the park and some deep breathing exercises later and you are still hungry, eat a light snack.

Additional tip: Eat before parties

Parties are food traps filled with your favorite high calorie food. During your 21-day challenge, you might find yourself in situations when it is difficult to make healthy food choices. To save yourself from jeopardizing all your efforts in weight loss, you have to prep yourself before you go to parties or gatherings where unhealthy food could be served.

Before you go to your party or gathering, have a few bites of healthy food from your meal plan. Drink a satisfying smoothie that will keep you full and hold of your hunger pangs as you go through the party's buffet table. This way, you won't binge eat while you are at the party.

Now that the 21 days are up, it's up to you to continue what you have been doing for the past weeks. Do not let all your good work in the last 21 days end just like that. Continue your healthy diet with healthy smoothies and exercise. Keep the habits that you developed.

Keep applying what you have learned in this book to all your daily activities. Once you have successfully adjusted to eating super foods and having smoothies as part of your daily diet, it will be easier for you to make healthy choices. Consequently, you will be able to lose the stubborn weight and fats that you have always wanted to shed.

Conclusion

Your weight loss success will depend on how determined you are to lose weight and how committed you are to stick to healthy eating habits. Keep following the tips in this book and you will see yourself losing 10, 20, 30 or more pounds.

Do not be too hard on yourself if you find yourself eating a donut or two. Just do not let yourself slip away and fall back to eating unhealthy again. You are only human with weaknesses just like everybody else. Condition yourself to have a smoothie instead when you feel like having sugary foods. Find a way to get back on track and follow the 21 day challenge again.

Part 2

Energy Smoothies

Energizer Smoothies

Prep Time: 4 Minutes
Servings: 6

Ingredients

- 2 gala apples, skin and seeds removed
- 2 cups almond milk
- 2 tablespoons of crushed almonds
- ½ teaspoon of cinnamon powder
- 2 teaspoons of crushed walnuts
- 1 teaspoon of almond butter
  Ice cubes, for chilling

Directions

1. Blend all the ingredients in a high-speed blender for 40 seconds.
2. Serve in smoothie glasses.
3. Enjoy chilled.

Supreme Smoothie

Prep Time: 5 Minutes
Servings: 6

Ingredients

- 2 mangoes, peeled and pits removed
- 4 ripped bananas, peeled
- 2 cups milk
- 2 green apples, seedless and cubed
- Ice cubes, for chilling
- 1/3 cup mint leaves, for garnishing

Directions

1. First wash all the fruits thoroughly.
2. Then peel the bananas and place it in a blender.
3. Next, peel and remove the pit of mangoes and dump the pulp into the blender.
4. Then add in the seedless apple chunks and mint leaves.
5. Pour in the milk.
6. Pulse until combined.
7. Pour into serving glasses.
8. Enjoy chilled.

Mango And Peach Smoothie

Prep Time: 5 Minutes
Servings: 6

Ingredients

- 2 mangos, peeled and diced
- 2 peaches, fresh and cubed
- 1/3 cup pumpkin seeds
- ½ cup almonds
- 2 cups of almond milk
- 1 cup ice cubes, for chilling

Directions

1. Combine all the listed ingredients in a blender and pulse until smooth.
2. Serve into glasses and enjoy.
3. Enjoy chilled.

Cocoa and Peanut Butter Smoothie

Prep Time: 6 Minutes
Servings: 7

Ingredients

- 2 cups almond milk, unsweetened
- 2 tablespoons of peanut butter, natural and organic
- 1 tablespoon of almonds, unsweetened
- 4 tablespoons of cocoa powder, unsweetened
- 3 tablespoons of honey
- 2 cups of ice cubes

Directions

1. Pour all the listed ingredients into a high-speed blender.
2. Blend for 30 seconds.
3. Once smooth, pour into serving glasses and enjoy.

Coffee Smoothie

Prep Time: 5 Minutes
Servings: 2

Ingredients

- 2 tablespoons of organic coffee beans
- 1 cup plain milk
- 2 tablespoons of flaxseed meal
- Ice cubes, for chilling
- 1 cup cold water, for brewing the coffee
- 2 tablespoons of brown sugar

Directions

1. Grind the coffee beans and brew the coffee in the brewer.
2. Next, pour the brewed coffee into the high-speed blender and add milk, flax meal, ice cubes, and sugar.
3. Blend for 30 seconds.
4. Pour it into the tall glasses.
5. Serve and enjoy immediately.

Super Food Smoothie

Berry Smoothie

Prep Time: 5 Minutes
Servings: 4

Ingredients

- 1 cup cranberry juice
- 4 strawberries, fresh
- 1 cup blueberries
- 1 cup Greek yogurt
- 4 tablespoons honey
- 1 cup crushed ice

Directions

1. Blend all the listed ingredients in the high-speed blender.
2. Once the smooth consistency is obtained, pour into glasses and enjoy.

Beetroot Smoothie

Prep Time: 5 Minutes
Servings: 2

Ingredients

- 2 cups fresh pineapple, chunks
- 2 cups Beetroot, washed
- 1 cup kale
- ½ teaspoon of lemon juice
- 4 tablespoons of honey
- 2 cups of ice cubes

Directions

1. Combine all the listed ingredients in the high-speed blender.
2. Pulse it for one minute.
3. Once the desired consistency obtained, pour into tall serving glasses.
4. Serve and enjoy.

Orange And Flax Seed Smoothie

Prep Time: 5 Minutes
Servings: 4

Ingredients

- 2 cups peaches, sliced
- 2 carrots, juice only
- 2 cups orange juice
- 2 tablespoons ground flax seeds
- 1-inch fresh ginger, chopped
- 2 gala apples, seedless and skinless
- 1 cup ice cubes for chilling

Directions

1. Combine all the listed ingredients in the blender.
2. Pulse it for 40 seconds.
3. Once the smooth consistency is obtained serve in tall glasses and enjoy.

Banana Nuts And Cocoa Smoothie

Prep Time: 5 Minutes
Servings: 4

Ingredients

- 2 cups of almond milk
- 4 bananas, ripped and peeled
- 1/3 cup of walnuts
- 1/3 almonds, chopped
- 2 tablespoons of honey
- ½ cup dates pits removed
- 2 teaspoons cocoa powder
- 1 cup ice cubes, for chilling

Directions

1. Peel the bananas and remove the pits from the dates.
2. Take a blender and combine all listed ingredients in it.
3. Blend for one minute at high speed.
4. Once the smooth consistency is obtained, serve into tall serving glasses and enjoy.

Avocado And Coconut Smoothie

Prep Time: 5 Minutes
Servings: 6

Ingredients

- 3 avocados, fresh and pitted
- 1 tablespoon of coconut oil
- 3 cups coconut milk
- 2 tablespoons of coconut flakes
- 1 teaspoon of sugar
- Ice cubes, for chilling

Directions

1. Pulse all the listed ingredients in a high-speed blender for one minute, until a smooth consistency is obtained.
2. Pour into serving glasses.
3. Enjoy.

Memory Booster Smoothies

Berry Medley

Prep Time: 5 Minutes
Servings: 4

Ingredients

- ½ cup strawberries
- 1 cup blueberries
- 1 cup raspberries
- 2 cups coconut milk
- 1 cup crushed ice cubes
- 1 tablespoon flax seeds

Directions

1. Combine strawberries, blueberries, raspberries, flax seeds and coconut milk in a blender.
2. Pulse it for 50 seconds at high speed.
3. Now add ice cubes to serving glasses and pour the smoothie into it.
4. Serve chilled and enjoy.

Dates And Walnuts Smoothie

Prep Time: 5 Minutes
Servings: 2

Ingredients

- 1 ripe banana, peeled
- 4 dates, pitted
- 1 tablespoon raw almond butter
- 1 tablespoon raw cacao powder
- ½ cup walnuts, grounded
- Ice cubes, for chilling

Directions

1. Blend all the listed ingredients in the high-speed blender.
2. Pour into tall smoothie glasses and enjoy.

Cantaloupe And Raw Egg Smoothie

Prep Time: 5 Minutes
Servings: 4

Ingredients

- 1 organic large egg, beaten lightly
- 1 cup Cantaloupe, fresh
- 2 teaspoons of sesame oil
- 2 cups milk
- 2 tablespoons of honey
- 1 teaspoon of flax seed
- Ice cubes, for chilling

Directions

1. First, blend egg in a blender until foamy.
2. Then add cantaloupe melon and oil.
3. Pulse it for a few seconds.
4. Next add milk, flax seeds, honey and ice cubes.
5. Blend it until smooth in consistency.
6. Next, pour it into serving glasses.
7. Enjoy.

Cleanse Smoothies

Go Green Smoothie

Prep Time: 4 Minutes
Servings: 3

Ingredients

- 2 carrots, peeled
- 4 cucumbers, peeled
- 1 cup parsley
- ½ cup of baby spinach
- 1 cup kale
- 1 lime, squeezed
- 1 cup water, filtered
- Pinch of salt

Directions

1. Wash all the vegetables before start making the smoothie.
2. Cut all the vegetables into small chunks.
3. Place all the vegetables with remaining listed ingredients into the high-speed blender.
4. Pulse it for 30 seconds.
5. Pour into serving glasses.
6. Serve and enjoy chilled by adding ice cubes.

Green Smoothie

Prep Time: 5 Minutes
Servings: 4

Ingredients

- 2 cups coconut water, cold
- 1 cup greens, roughly chopped
- A handful of parsley
- A handful of cilantro
- 1 cucumber, diced
- 6 green apples, cored and diced
- 1 cup diced peaches
- Ice cubes, for chilling

Directions

1. Add all the listed ingredients into the high-speed blender.
2. Pulse it until smooth.
3. Pour into the serving glasses.
4. Enjoy.

Best Cleanse Smoothie

Prep Time: 5 Minutes
Servings: 5

Ingredients

- 1 stalks kale, stem removed
- 1 cup baby spinach
- 1 lemon, seeds removed and peeled
- 1-inch ginger, peeled
- 1 cucumber, peeled and diced
- A Handful of fresh parsley
- 6 pears, chopped
- 2 green apples, seeds removed
- 2 cups water
- Ice cubes, for chilling

Directions

1. Add all the listed ingredients into the high-speed blender.
2. Pulse it until smooth.
3. Pour into the serving glasses.
4. Enjoy.

Kale Smoothie

Prep Time: 5 Minutes
Servings: 6

Ingredients

- 1 cup cherries
- 2 cups of kale, stem removed
- 2 cups water
- 4 teaspoons of hemp seeds
- 1 cup ice cubes
- 1/3 cup blueberries

Directions

1. Add all the listed ingredients into the high-speed blender.
2. Pulse it until smooth.
3. Pour into the serving glasses.
4. Enjoy.

Detoxifying Smoothie

Prep Time: 5 Minutes
Servings: 4

Preparation Time: 5 Minutes
Yield: 5 Servings

Ingredients

- 1 apple, peeled, de-seeded and cubed
- 2 cups grapes
- 4 sticks of celery
- 2 cups kale
- Ice cubes, for chilling
- 1 cup water

Directions

1. Add all the listed ingredients into the high-speed blender.
2. Pulse until the desired consistency is obtained.
3. Pour into tall serving glasses.
4. Enjoy chilled.

Low Sugar/Diabetic Smoothies

Diabetic Smoothie

Prep Time: 5 Minutes
Servings: 4

Ingredients

- 1 cup strawberries, chopped
- 1 cup unsweetened almond milk
- 1 cup Greek-style yogurt, low fat
- 1 cup ice cubes, for chilling

Directions

1. Place all ingredients in a blender.
2. Pulse until the desired consistency is obtained.
3. Pour into tall serving glasses.
4. Enjoy chilled.

Low Carb Green Smoothie

Prep Time: 5 Minutes
Servings: 4

Ingredients

- 1 cup water
- 1 gala apple, cut into cubes and seeds discarded
- 1 green pear, cut into chunks
- 2 cups spinach
- 20 Moscato grapes
- 2 tablespoons agave nectar, or to taste
- Ice cubes, for chilling

Directions

1. Place all ingredients in a blender.
2. Pulse until the desired consistency is obtained.
3. Pour into tall serving glasses.
4. Enjoy chilled.

Diabetic Oatmeal Smoothie

Prep Time: 5 Minutes
Servings: 5

Ingredients

- 1 cup uncooked oats, grounded
- ½ ripe banana, peeled
- 3 cups almond milk, unsweetened
- 2 tablespoons of ground flax-seed
- 4 teaspoons of stevia
- 2 teaspoons of coffee extract

Directions

1. Combine all ingredients in a high-speed blender and pulse for 30 seconds
2. Pour into tall serving glasses and enjoy.

Pineapple And Spinach Smoothie

Prep Time: 5 Minutes
Servings: 4

Ingredients

- 1 cup water
- 1 cup pineapple, chunks
- 2 cups baby spinach
- ½ cup celery sticks
- 1 green apple, chopped and seeds removed
- 1 tablespoon of stevia, to taste
- Ice cubes for chilling

Directions

1. Add all the listed ingredients into the blender.
2. Pulse until a smooth consistency is obtained.
3. Pour into the ice-filled serving glasses.
4. Enjoy.

Peach Smoothie For Dietetics

Prep Time: 5 Minutes
Servings: 4

Ingredients

- 1 peach, peeled, pitted, and chopped
- 1 cup plain milk
- 1 cup Greek yogurt
- 1 cup ice cubes
- ½ teaspoon of ground cinnamon, or to taste
- 2 scoops of stevia, or to taste

Directions

1. Place milk, peach Greek yogurt, ice cube, stevia and cinnamon in the blender.
2. Pulse it until smooth.
3. Pour into serving glasses and enjoy.

Dessert Smoothies

Apple Dessert Smoothie

Prep Time: 5 Minutes
Servings: 2

Ingredients

- 1 cup of apples, stewed
- 1/3 teaspoon of cinnamon powder, or to taste
- ½ cup of vanilla ice cream
- 2 oatmeal cookies, crumbled
- 1 cup milk

Directions

1. Place all ingredients into your blender.
2. Blend for a few seconds until all ingredients combined into a smooth consistency
3. Pour into ice-filled serving glasses and enjoy.

Caramel Smoothie

Prep Time: 5 Minutes
Servings: 4

Ingredients

- 1 cup whole milk
- 1 scoop of chocolate ice cream
- 1 scoop of vanilla ice cream
- 2 tablespoons of dark chocolate chips, unsweetened
- 1 tablespoon of butterscotch sauce
- Handful of peanuts

Directions

1. Place milk, chocolate ice-cream, vanilla ice-cream, chocolate chips, butterscotch sauce and peanuts into your blender.
2. Blend for a few seconds until all ingredients combined into a smooth consistency.
3. Pour into ice-filled serving glasses and enjoy.

Key Lime Yoplait Smoothie Recipe

Prep Time: 5 Minutes
Servings: 2

Ingredients

- 1 cup fat-free Key lime pie yogurt
- 1 ripe banana, sliced
- ½ cup organic milk
- 1 tablespoon lime juice
- 1/4 teaspoon of dry lemon lime-flavored soft drink powder
- 1 cup vanilla frozen yogurt

Directions

1. Pulse all ingredients except frozen yogurt into your high-speed blender.
2. Pour into tall ice-filled servings glasses.
3. Serve with a dollop of frozen yogurt on top.

Peanut Butter Smoothie

Prep Time: 5 Minutes
Servings: 4

Ingredients

- 3 frozen bananas
- 1 tablespoon cocoa powder
- 1 tablespoons peanut butter
- 1 cup almond milk
- 1/3 teaspoon vanilla extract

Directions

1. Add all the listed ingredients into the blender.
2. Pulse it until smooth.
3. Serve into glasses and enjoy.

Oreo Smoothie

Prep Time: 5 Minutes
Servings: 1

Ingredients

- 1 cup Vanilla ice cream
- ½ Cup Milk, low fat
- 7 Oreo cookies, crushed

Directions

1. Add all the listed ingredients into the blender.
2. Pulse it until smooth.
3. Serve into glasses and enjoy.

Dairy Free Smoothies

Sunshine Smoothie

Prep Time: 5 Minutes
Servings: 4

Ingredients

- 2 cups coconut milk
- 4 bananas, peeled, sliced
- 1 cup of mango, flesh
- 1 cup strawberries
- Ice cubes for chilling

Directions

1. Combine all the listed ingredients in a high-speed blender.
2. Blend until smooth.
3. Serve and enjoy.

Granny Smith Apples Smoothie

Prep Time: 5 Minutes
Servings: 4

Ingredients

- 1 cup spinach, washed
- 1 cup kale
- 4 granny smith apples, peeled and cored
- 1 cup purified water

Directions

1. Place all the listed ingredients in a blender.
2. Blend until smooth.
3. Serve into glasses and enjoy.

Banana And Nuts Smoothie

Prep Time: 5 Minutes
Servings: 4

Ingredients

- 1/3 cup of walnuts, crushed
- ½ cup almonds, crushed
- 1 cup oats, soaked overnight
- 1 cup of almond milk
- 2 bananas
- 4 dates, pitted
- Ice cubes, for chilling

Directions

1. Combine all the listed ingredients in your blender.
2. Pulse it until smooth.
3. Serve into glasses and enjoy.

Pineapple And Avocado Smoothie

Prep Time: 5 Minutes
Servings: 4

Ingredients

- 1 cup pineapple
- 2 avocados, cored and peeled
- 2 cups coconut milk
- Ice cubes, for chilling

Directions

1. Combine all the listed ingredients in a high-speed blender.
2. Blend until smooth consistency.
3. Serve into glasses.
4. Enjoy.

Soymilk Smoothie

Prep Time: 5 Minutes
Servings: 4

Ingredients

- ½ cup almond butter
- 1 cup strawberries
- 1 cup soy milk, unsweetened
- 1 cup ice cubes

Directions

1. Combine all the listed ingredients in a blender.
2. Blend until smooth consistency is obtained.
3. Serve into tall glasses and enjoy chilled.

Cocoa And Macadamia Smoothie

Prep Time: 5 Minutes
Servings: 4

Ingredients

- 2 tablespoons of honey, or to taste
- 4 tablespoons macadamia nuts, crushed
- 1 tablespoon of cocoa powder
- 2 cups coconut milk
- 1 cup ice cubes

Directions

1. Add all the listed ingredients in a blender.
2. Pulse it until smooth.
3. Serve in smoothie glasses and enjoy.

Ketogenic Smoothies

Peanut Butter Caramel Milkshake

Prep Time: 5 Minutes
Servings: 3

Ingredients

- 1 cup ice cubes
- 2 cups coconut milk, unsweetened
- 4 tablespoons peanut butter
- 4 tablespoons Salted Caramel
- 1 teaspoon **xanthan gum**
- 2 tablespoons **MCT oil**

Directions

1. Add all the listed ingredients in a blender.
2. Pulse it until smooth.
3. Serve in smoothie glasses and enjoy.

Blueberry Smoothie

Prep Time: 5 Minutes
Servings: 4

Ingredients

- 2 tablespoons **flaxseed meal**
- 2 tablespoons **Chia seeds**
- 2 cups unsweetened coconut milk
- Few drops of stevia
- ½ cup blueberries
- 2 tablespoons **MCT oil**
- ¼ teaspoon **xanthan gum**

Directions

1. Add all the listed ingredients in a blender.
2. Pulse it until smooth.
3. Serve into ice-filled smoothie glasses and enjoy.

Blackberry Chocolate Smoothie

Prep Time: 5 Minutes
Servings: 2

Ingredients

- 1 cup coconut milk
- ½ cup blackberries
- 1 tablespoon of cocoa powder
- Few drops of stevia
- 1 teaspoon of xanthan gum
- 1 cup ice cubes

Directions

1. Add all the listed ingredients in a blender.
2. Pulse it until smooth.
3. Serve in smoothie glasses and enjoy.

Cherry Vanilla Smoothie

Prep Time: 5 Minutes
Servings: 4

Ingredients

- ½ cup full-fat canned coconut milk
- ½ cup water, filtered
- 1/6 teaspoon pure vanilla powder
- Sea salt, pinch
- 1 cup organic sweet cherries
- 1 cup ice cubes

Directions

1. Add all the listed ingredients in a blender.
2. Pulse it until smooth.
3. Serve in smoothie glasses and enjoy.

Keto Strawberry Milkshake

Prep Time: 4 Minutes
Servings: 4

Ingredients

- ½ cup coconut milk
- ½ cup heavy whipping cream
- Ice cubes, for chilling
- 2 tablespoons Strawberries
- 2 tablespoons MCT oil
- 1/3 teaspoon xanthan gum

Directions

1. Add all the listed ingredients in a blender.
2. Pulse it until smooth.
3. Serve in smoothie glasses and enjoy.

High Protein Smoothie

Pomegranate And Beetroot Smoothie

Prep Time: 5 Minutes
Servings: 4

Ingredients

- 1 cup beet-root, peeled
- 1 cup Greek yogurt
- 1 cup pomegranate juice
- 2 teaspoons honey
- Ice cubes, for chilling

Directions

1. Add all the listed ingredients into the blender
2. Blend for 30 seconds.
3. Once the desired consistency obtained, pour into tall glasses and enjoy.
4. Serve and enjoy.

Raspberry Almond Chia Smoothie

Prep Time: 5 Minutes
Servings: 4

Ingredients

- 1 cup plain Greek yogurt
- 2/3 cup almond milk
- ½ cup raspberries, frozen
- 1/4 cup almonds, divided
- 2 tablespoons honey
- 1 tablespoon of Chia seeds

Directions

1. Add all the listed ingredients in a blender.
2. Pulse it until smooth.
3. Serve in smoothie glasses and enjoy.

Peanut Butter And Jelly Smoothie

Prep Time: 5 Minutes
Servings: 4

Ingredients

- 1 cup of non-fat Greek yogurt
- ½ cup almond milk, unsweetened
- 2 scoops stevia
- 25 green grapes
- ½ cup peanut flour
- Ice cubes, for chilling
- 1 tablespoon of protein powder

Directions

1. First, add Greek yogurt, almond milk, stevia, and grapes in a blender.
2. Pulse it for a few seconds.
3. Then add peanut flour, protein powder, and ice cubes.
4. Pulse until a smooth consistency is obtained.
5. Enjoy.

Green Banana Smoothie

Prep Time: 5 Minutes
Servings: 4

Ingredients

- 1 large banana, peeled, frozen
- 1 cup Greek yogurt
- 1 cup almond milk, unsweetened
- 2 cups baby spinach
- 1/3 teaspoon vanilla extract
- 2tablespoons almond butter
- 1 teaspoon of protein powder

Directions

1. Add all the listed ingredients in a blender.
2. Pulse it until smooth.
3. Serve in smoothie glasses and enjoy.

Very Berry Smoothie

Prep Time: 5 Minutes
Servings: 4

Ingredients

- 2 cups water
- 2 cups spinach
- 2 cups mixed berries, frozen
- ½ cup yogurt
- 2 scoops vanilla protein powder
- 1 tablespoon of walnuts, grounded
- 1 teaspoon of flaxseed, grounded

Directions

1. Add all the listed ingredients in a blender.
2. Pulse it until smooth.
3. Serve in smoothie glasses and enjoy.

Smoothies For Gout & Arthritis

Smoothie To Help With Gout

Prep Time: 5 Minutes
Servings: 4

Ingredients

- 1-1/2 cup of water
- 1 cup pineapple, cubed
- 1 orange, peeled and deseeded
- 1 carrot, chopped
- 1 tablespoon Chia seeds
- 1-inch fresh ginger
- Handfuls of baby spinach

Directions

1. Add all the listed ingredients into the blender.
2. Pulse it until smooth.
3. Serve into glasses and enjoy

Kiwi And Kale Smoothie

Prep Time: 5 Minutes
Servings: 4

Ingredients

- 1 cup of water, filtered
- 2 mangoes, peeled and pitted
- 2 kiwi fruits, peeled
- 1 cup kale, torn into pieces

Directions

1. Pulse all the ingredients in a blender until smooth.
2. Serve into ice-filled glasses and enjoy.

Melon-Mango Smoothie

Prep Time: 5 Minutes
Servings: 4

Ingredients

- 1 cup of filtered water
- 1 cup cantaloupe, cubed
- 2 mangos, peeled and pitted
- 4 large strawberries
- 2 cups baby spinach, washed

Directions

1. Pulse all the ingredients in blender until smooth
2. Serve into ice-filled glasses and enjoy.

Strawberry-Orange Smoothie

Prep Time: 5 Minutes
Servings: 4

Ingredients

- 1 cup of filtered water
- 2 bananas, peeled and sliced
- 6 strawberries
- 2 oranges, de-seeded
- Ice cubes, for chilling

Directions

1. Pulse all the ingredients in a blender until smooth.
2. Serve into ice-filled glasses and enjoy.

Grapefruit Smoothie

Prep Time: 3 Minutes
Servings:4

Ingredients

- 1 cup filtered water
- 1 fresh banana, peeled and sliced
- 1 red grapefruit, peeled and seedless
- 1 cup pineapple, cubed
- ½ cup fresh parsley

Directions

1. Pulse all the listed ingredients in a high-speed blender for one minute.
2. Pour into ice-filled serving glasses.
3. Serve and enjoy.

Best Smoothies By Blood Type

Smoothie For Type A Blood Type

Prep Time: Minutes
Servings: 4

Ingredients

- 2 scoops Protein Blend Powder A
- 1 cup water
- ½ cup soy milk
- 1 cup of blackberries

Directions

1. Pulse all the listed ingredients in a high-speed blender for one minute.
2. Pulse until a smooth consistency is obtained.
3. Pour into ice-filled serving glasses.
4. Serve and enjoy.

Smoothie For Type B Blood Type

Prep Time: 5 Minutes
Servings: 4

Ingredients

- 1 cup strawberries
- 1 banana
- ½ cup low-fat yogurt
- 1 cup milk
- 1 cup grape juice
- 3 teaspoons honey

Directions

1. Pulse all the listed ingredients in a high-speed blender for one minute.
2. Pulse until a smooth consistency is obtained.
3. Pour into ice-filled serving glasses.
4. Serve and enjoy.

Smoothie For Type Ab Blood Type

Prep Time: 5 Minutes
Servings: 2

Ingredients

- 4 carrots, peeled
- 1 cup grapes
- 1 cup rice milk
- 4 tablespoons of Agave syrup, or to taste
- 1 cup ice cubes, for chilling

Directions

1. Place all ingredients in a blender.
2. Pulse until the desired consistency is obtained.
3. Pour into tall serving glasses.
4. Enjoy chilled.

Smoothie For Type O Blood Type

Prep Time: 5 Minutes
Servings: 4

Ingredients

- 2 scoops Protein powder
- 1 cup water
- 1 cup almond milk
- 1 ripe banana, peeled
- 1 cup of blueberries
- 1 cup cherries
- ½ cup pineapple, cut into small chunks

Directions

1. Combine all the listed ingredients in a blender.
2. Pulse it until smooth.
3. Serve into ice-filled glasses and enjoy.
4. Enjoy chilled.

Berry Coconut Smoothie

Ingredients

1/2 cup frozen blueberries

1 tbsp almond butter

1 tbsp unsweetened flaked coconut

1/2 cup water or as needed

Preparation

Blend until smooth serve cold

Island Dream Smoothie

Ingredients

1 banana

1/2 cup Frozen mango pieces

1/3 cup plain yogurt

1/2 cup orange mango juice

Preparation

Blend until smooth and enjoy!

Smoothie A La Orange

Ingredients

1 cup milk

1 cup of ice water

16 oz can of frozen orange juice from concentrate

12 ice cubes

1/4 teaspoon vanilla extract

1/8 cup white sugar

Preparation

blend and enjoy

Creamy Lime Chiller

Ingredients

1 cup milk

1 cup lime sherbet

1/4 cup limeade concentrate

yellow food coloring optional

Preparation

Blend until smooth

Pour into chilled glasses

Serve immediately

Summer's Bliss Smoothie

Ingredients

1/3 cup lemon juice

1/3 cup sugar

2 cups cubed seedless watermelon

2 cups fresh strawberries

2 cups Ice Cubes

Preparation

Put the lemon juice, sugar, strawberries and watermelon into the blender.

Blend until smooth

Add ice and blend until it's a slushy consistency.

Serve immediately

Enjoy

Java Chiller Smoothie

Ingredients

1 cup milk 1/2 cup Nutella hazelnut spread

4 teaspoons instant espresso powder

6 Ice Cube's

2 cups vanilla ice cream

Preparation

chocolate curls optional

In blender combine milk Nutella and espresso powder

Blend until smooth and Ice blend until smooth

add ice cream

Blend until smooth

Pouring into chilled glasses and enjoy!

Chunky Monkey Smoothie

Ingredients

2 bananas

2 tablespoons cocoa powder

3/4 cup ice

1/4 cup creamy peanut butter

1/2 cup milk

1/2 cup vanilla low-fat Greek yogurt

BLEND AND ENJOY!

Pineapple Mango Smoothie

INGREDIENTS

1 Cup Milk, soy milk or almond milk

1 Cup Frozen Pineapple

2 Cup Frozen Mango

2 Cup Spinach

PREPARATION

Pour milk into a blender.

Add pineapple, mango, and spinach.

Cover with blender lid and blend to combine.

If blender stops turning, add a little more milk.

If desired add a couple of ice cubes to make the smoothie very cold and icy.

Serve and Enjoy!

Cookies And Cream Smoothie

Ingredients

10 Oreo cookies or any chocolate cookies, crumbled
2 cups vanilla ice cream, softened
1/4 cup low-fat milk
3 tablespoons chocolate syrup

Preparation

In a blender, combine milk, ice cream and chocolate syrup.
Add 1/2 of crumbled cookies then process until blended.
 Pour into glasses then sprinkle with remaining cookies then serve immediately.

Carrot Smoothie

INGREDIENTS

3 pieces medium-sized carrots, peeled and cut into cubes

sugar or other sweetener to taste

1 cup ice cubes

1/2 cup powdered milk(optional)

PREPARATION

1. In a blender, process carrots, milk, and sugar until blended.
2. Add ice and blend until smooth, add more sugar if needed.
3. Pour into glasses then served cold.

Green Mango Shake

INGREDIENTS

2 green mangoes, peeled and cut into cubes
1/2 cup powdered milk(optional)
2 tablespoons sugar or other sweetener to taste
1 cup ice cubes

PREPARATION

1. In a blender, process green mango, milk, and sugar until blended.
2. Add ice and blend until smooth, add more sugar if needed.
3. Pour into glasses then served cold.

Cocoa Cream Smoothie

Ingredients:
- 3/4 cup chocolate powder
- 3 tablespoons sugar
- 3-4 cup ice cubes
- 1/2 cup water
- vanilla ice cream
- toppings(rice crispy, chocolate or rainbow sprinkles, marshmallow)

Preparation

1. In a blender, process chocolate powder, sugar and water until blended.
2. Add ice and blend until smooth, add more sugar if needed.
3. Pour into glasses then top with a scoop of vanilla ice cream.
4. Sprinkle with remaining chocolate powder and rainbow sprinkle. Enjoy!

Strawberry Smoothie

Ingredients:

400 grams fresh strawberries
2 cups yogurt or ice cream(vanilla/strawberry flavor)
1 cup fresh milk
1 cup ice cubes
1/4 cup white sugar

Preparation

1. In a blender, process strawberries, milk, and ice cream until blended.
2. Add ice and sugar then blend until smooth, add more sugar if needed.
3. Pour into glasses then garnish with fresh strawberry. Serve cold.

Notes:
1. You may also use yogurt as alternative to ice cream.

Mixed Fruit Shake

Ingredients:

2 cups mixed fruits, cut into cubes(I used watermelon, avocado, pineapple)
3 tablespoons sugar or any sweetener
1/4 cup fresh milk
1 cup ice cubes

Preparation

1. In a blender, combine fruits, milk and sugar then process until blended.
2. Add ice and blend until smooth, add more sugar if needed.
3. Pour into glasses then served cold.

Clean Breeze Smoothie

INGREDIENTS

1 small cucumber, chopped

2 ripe kiwis, peeled

1/2 cup low-fat plain Greek yogurt

2 tablespoons fresh cilantro leaves

6 ice cubes

PREPARATION

Combine cucumber, kiwis, yogurt, cilantro and ice cubes in blender; blend until smooth. Serve immediately.

Sunburst Smoothie

Ingredients

3/4 cup frozen pineapple cubes

3/4 cup frozen mango cubes

3/4 cup 100% orange juice

1 banana

1 Tbsp chia seeds

Preparation

Add a handful of spinach (optional - only add if you want to make it green)

Blend together all ingredients until smooth and creamy. To make half of it green: Pour half of the orange mixture into several glasses. Mix the remainder with a big handful of spinach. Blend until smooth. Pour over the orange mixture and serve!

Avocado Smoothie

Ingredients

3 medium sized avocados

24 ice cubes

1 cup condensed milk

1½ cup full cream milk

Preparation

Place all ingredients in a blender, blend until completely smooth.

Place in glass, serve and consume immediately.

Classic Fruit And Yogurt Smoothie

Ingredients:

1/2 cup of your child's favorite fruit, such as peaches, bananas, pineapples, strawberries, mango, etc.

3/4 cup of yogurt

1 cup milk

2 cups ice

Preparation

Cut all fruit into chunks

Place all ingredients into a blender and puree until smooth. A refreshing treat in minutes.

Peaches and Cream Smoothie

Peaches N Cream Smoothie

Ingredients:

1 cup evaporated milk

1 tablespoon sugar

1 cup vanilla yogurt

2 fresh peaches, washed and sliced (seed removed)

Preparation

Blend until smooth to desired consistency and serve.

Strawberry Banana Smoothie

Ingredients:

3 Bananas

4 cups frozen strawberries

2 cups orange juice

4 cups ice

Preparation

Blend all ingredients together and serve.

1.1 Morning Glory Smoothie

This morning smoothie is heart and healthy and sets you up to face the whole day ahead!
Serves - 2
Time - 5 minutes
Ingredients:
1 ripe Banana
1 cup of Ripe Mango, diced
½ an Avocado, diced
1 cup of Soy milk
2 Tbsp of whole Flax Seeds
Method:
Add all the ingredients into a blender and blend until smooth and creamy!

1.2 Wake Me Up Smoothie!

This smoothie is tasty and will recharge your batteries. This smoothie can easily be substituted for a glorious breakfast!

Serves – 2

Time – 5 minutes

Ingredients:

1 cup of Strawberries (fresh or frozen)

1 cup of fresh Papaya, cubed

1 Orange, peeled and sectioned

½ of a ripe Avocado

1 cup of Vanilla flavored Yoghurt

Method:

Blend all the ingredients in a blender and blend until smooth and creamy!

1.3 Pomegranate-Banana Oats Morning Smoothie

This smoothie is super sweet and satisfying! This is a complete meal in itself!

Serves – 2
Time – 5 Minutes

Ingredients:
1 cup of Pomegranate seeds

1 ripe Banana

1 cup of Rolled oats

4-5 Almonds

2 cups of low fat Yoghurt/milk

Method:
Bend all the ingredients until smooth and creamy! Enjoy!

1.4 Avocado and Agave nectar smoothie

Super healthy, super delicious and super satisfying! This smoothie is an excellent start to the day!

Serves – 2

Time – 5 minutes

Ingredients:
1 ripe Avocado

1 Banana

1 cup of fresh Vanilla flavored Yoghurt

1 cup of Coconut Meat

1 Tbsp of Agave Nectar

1 Tbsp Sunflower Seeds

Method:
Blend all the ingredients until smooth and super creamy! Enjoy!

1.5 Banana and Yogurt-Granola Smoothie

This is one of most familiar breakfast recipes, only this time it is in the form of a smoothie! This is a perfect breakfast if you are on-the-go!

Serves – 2

Time – 5 Minutes

Ingredients:
1 ripe Banana

1 cup of your favorite Granola

2 cups of Vanilla Yoghurt

5-6 Almonds

Method:
Blend all the ingredients in a blender until smooth and creamy! Enjoy!

1.6 Supercharge Morning Smoothie

This smoothie lives up to its name. It will awaken you and prepare you for the rest of the day!

Serves – 2
Time – 5 minutes

Ingredients:
1 cup of fresh Pineapple, cubed

1 cup of Watermelon, cubed

1 Green Apple, diced

2 handfuls of Baby Spinach

2 Tbsp Sunflower Seeds

Method:
Blend all the ingredients into a blender and blend until smooth! Serve immediately!

1.7 Peaches and Coconut Smoothie

This sweet and creamy smoothie is bright and healthy way to start your day. You can add nuts and seeds of your choice to make this a complete and filling breakfast!

Serves-2

Time- 5 Minutes

Ingredients:

2-3 fresh Peaches, chopped

1 cup of Coconut Meat

2 cups of Coconut Milk

1 scoop of Vanilla Protein powder

1 Tbsp Agave Nectar

1 Tsp Nutmeg powder

Method:
Blend all the ingredients until smooth. Serve immediately!

1.8 Minty Mango- Soy Milk Smoothie

This refreshing mango smoothie is sweet and delicious. It is a very healthy take on a regular mango smoothie!

Serves – 2

Time – 5 Minutes

Ingredients:
2 cups of fresh Mango, chopped

2 cups of Soy Milk

Few sprigs of Mint

1 Tbsp whole Flaxseeds

Method:
Blend all the ingredients until smooth and delicious. Enjoy!

1.9 Raspberry-Pistachio and Goji Berry -Oats Smoothie

This smoothie is full of anti-oxidants which is great for maintaining food health. This delicious smoothie is what makes for great mornings!

Serves – 2

Time – 5 Minutes

Ingredients:

2 cups of raspberries

½ cup of goji berries

1 cup of oats

½ cup of pistachios

1 cup of almond milk

Method:
Blend all the ingredients until smooth and creamy! Enjoy!

1.10 Blueberry Almond-Muesli Smoothie

This blueberry morning smoothie with almonds and smoothie is like a breakfast in a glass! It is a complete meal in its own right!

Serves – 2

Time – 5 Minutes

Ingredients:
1 cup of blueberries

1 cup of muesli

1/2 cup of almonds

1 cup of almond milk

2 Tbsp whole flaxseeds

Method:
Blend all the ingredients in a blender and blend until smooth and creamy! Serve immediately!

2.1 Pomegranate and Wild Mulberry Smoothie

This smoothie is super charged with anti-oxidants and anti-ageing benefits that instantly boost your energy!

Serves – 2

Time – 5 Minutes

Ingredients:

1 cup of Pomegranate seeds

1 cup of wild mulberry (black or red)

2 cups of fresh lemonade

Method:

Blend all the ingredients into a blender until smooth. Enjoy chilled!

2.2 Spinach and Mixed berry Smoothie

This smoothie is jam packed with anti-oxidants from the berries and iron rich goodness from the spinach that will definitely energize you!

Serves – 2

Time – 5 Minutes

Ingredients:
1 handful of Baby Spinach

½ cup of Raspberry

½ cup of Blueberry

1 cup of low fat Buttermilk

Honey to taste

Method:
Blend all the ingredients into a blender and blend until smooth and creamy!

2.3 Beetroot, Apple-Blackberry Smoothie

Beetroots are a good source of vitamins and minerals and have great anti-inflammatory benefits. This smoothie is great to taste with the apple-blackberry combo!

Serves – 2
Time – 5 Minutes

Ingredients:
½ a medium Beetroot (cleaned and peeled)

1 Apple

1 cup of Blackberries

1 cup of Coconut Milk

Method:
Beetroot is difficult to blend so it is easier to chop them before adding into the blender. Blend all the ingredients in a blender until smooth. Enjoy!

2.4 Kiwi- Pineapple Green Tea Smoothie

Green tea contains amazing anti-oxidant properties. Kiwi and pineapple add even more anti-oxidant properties making this smoothie an anti-oxidant powerhouse!

Serves – 2
Time – 5 Minutes

Ingredients:
2 Kiwis, fresh and peeled

1 cup Pineapple cubes

½ cup of brewed, strong Green tea, cooled

1 Banana

Method:
Blend all the ingredients into a blend and process until smooth and creamy

2.5 Cucumber, Red bell Pepper and Pear Smoothie

This smoothie is hydrating, sweet-zingy and has great health benefits. This is a great way to incorporate and experience the best these veggies have to offer!

Serve – 2

Time – 5 Minutes

Ingredients:
1 large Cucumber

1 Red Bell Pepper, deseeded and cleaned

2 Pears

A small knob of Ginger

Method:
Blend all the ingredients into a blender and process until smooth. Serve immediately. Enjoy!

2.6 Avocado and Banana Smoothie

This smoothie is packed with good nutrients and fibre. This smoothie will keep you energized for a long time!

Serves – 2

Time – 5 Minutes

Ingredients:

1 Avocado

1 Banana

2 cups of Coconut water

A small knob of Ginger

Method:
Blend all the ingredients until its creamy! Enjoy!

2.7 Beetroot and Watermelon Smoothie

This smoothie is a great looker! It is a vivid pinkish-red and it is both hydrating and energizing!

Serves – 2

Time – 5 Minutes

Ingredients
½ a medium Beetroot

2 ½ cups of Watermelon cubes

A small knob of Ginger

Method:
Blend all the ingredients into the blender and blend for 20-30 seconds. Serve immediately!

2.8 Carrot, Tomato and Apple Smoothie

This is a perfectly orange and perfectly tasty smoothie. Again, loaded with a lot of vitamins and minerals, this smoothie will keep you satisfied and energized for a long time!

Serves – 2

Time – 5 Minutes

Ingredients:
2 Carrots, peeled and cubed

2 cups of chopped, fresh Tomato

2 Apples

Method:
Blend all the ingredients in a blender and serve immediately. Enjoy!

2.9 The Orange Delight

This smoothie is called as the orange delight as both carrots and oranges-the main heroes of this smoothie are bright orange in colour. The orange is rich in vitamin C white carrots are rich in vitamin A!

Serves – 2

Time – 5 Minutes

Ingredients:
3 Carrots, peeled

2 Oranges

Ice cubes (optional)

A small knob of Ginger

Method:
Blend all the ingredients until smooth and juicy! Enjoy!

2.10 The Green Monster

This smoothie is a gorgeous green thanks to the kale, cucumber and green apple in it! This smoothie not only tastes great but it is really healthy and energizing!

Serves – 2

Time – 5 Minutes

Ingredients:
A handful of Kale leaves, stems removed

1 Green Apple

1 Cucumber

1 cup of Lemonade

A small knob of Ginger

Mint leaves (optional)

Method:
Blend all the ingredients until smooth. Serve immediately. Enjoy!

3.1 Citrusy Spinach and Mango Delight

This smoothie has amazing health benefits which are great for maintaining good skin as well.

Serves – 2

Time – 5 Minutes

Ingredients:
2 handfuls of Baby Spinach

1 cup of fresh Mango, diced

½ Avocado, diced

1 whole Lemon, rind removed

1 Tbsp whole Flaxseeds

1 Tbsp Agave Nectar

Method:
Blend all the ingredients in the blender until smooth and creamy. Serve immediately. Enjoy!

3.2 The Anti oxidant Surprise

All the ingredients in this smoothie do wonders for your skin and completion.

Serves – 2

Time – 5 Minutes

Ingredients:
2 Carrots, peeled and cut

1 Tomato, diced

1 ½ cup of strong Chinese Green Tea

A handful of Walnuts

1 Tbsp. Wild Honey

Method:
Blend all the ingredients until smooth. Serve over ice! Enjoy!

3.3 Beautiful Complexion Smoothie

Proteins are building blocks of the body. Therefore protein is important when you are trying to improve complexion as well. This smoothie is a great way to incorporate tofu- protein in your diet!

Serves – 2

Time – 5 Minutes

Ingredients:
½ cup of soft Tofu

1 Orange, peeled and sectioned

1 cup Mango

3 leaves of Dinosaur Kale

1 cup of Butter Milk

Method:
Blend all the ingredients in the blender until smooth. Enjoy!

3.4 The Vitamin C Surprise

This smoothie is loaded with Vitamin C which is an essential for good, even and glowing complexion!

Serves – 2

Time – 5 Minutes

Ingredients:
1 Yellow Bell Pepper, deseeded

2 Kiwis, peeled and cut

1 Lemon, rind removed

1 Tbsp. Goji berries

1 Tbsp Maple Syrup

Method:
Blend all the ingredients into a blender and blend until smooth. Enjoy*!*

3.5 The Sunny Smoothie

This smoothie is sure to remind you of the sun! This sunny delight is packed with essential ingredients needed to make you glow from within!

Serves – 2

Time – 5 Minutes

Ingredients:
1 cup of Pumpkin, chopped

2 Carrots, peeled and cut

1 Orange, peeled and sectioned

1 Tbsp. Sunflower Seeds

Method:
Blend all the ingredients into a blender and blend until smooth and creamy! Enjoy!

3.6 Blueberry and Passion Fruit Oats Smoothie

This is a tasty and elegant smoothie that can double as a dessert! What is great is that this smoothie offers amazing skin benefits thanks to the skin-friendly ingredients!

Serves – 2

Time – 5 Minutes

Ingredients:
1 cup of Blueberry (frozen/ fresh)

2 Passion Fruit, halved

1 cup of Whole Oats

1 ½ cup Coconut Milk

1 Tbsp. cold pressed Flaxseed oil

Honey if required

Method:
Blend all the ingredients into a blender and blend until smooth and creamy! Serve immediately.

3.7 Dragon Fruit and Swiss-Chard almond Smoothie

This smoothie features the best ingredients required to hydrate and moisturise your skin. Dragonfruit, Chard leaves and Lemon juice refresh the skin, and improve its ability to heal, making your skin glow from the inside out.

Serves – 2

Time – 5 Minutes

Ingredients:
1 Dragon fruit, peeled and cut

3-4 Swiss chard leaves and stems

2 cups of Almond milk

1 scoop of Protein powder

2 tsp Lemon juice

Few Mint leaves

A Pinch of salt

Method:
Blend all the ingredients until smooth and creamy! Serve immediately.

3.8 Fabulous Skin Smoothie

This smoothie has ingredients that benefit and enhance the complexion and make it glow. This smoothie is a great way to incorporate greens in your diet!

Serves – 2

Time – 5 Minutes

Ingredients:
2 large collard leaves

2-3 leaves of swiss chard

1 cup of strawberries

2 apples, diced

1 lemon, rind removed

Method:
Blend all the ingredients until smooth and creamy! Enjoy!

3.9 Pink in your cheeks Smoothie

This gorgeous smoothie will put the pink back in your cheeks! It's a great complexion booster.

Serves – 2

Time – 5 Minutes

Ingredients:
2 medium Tomatoes, diced

1 red bell Pepper, deseeded

1 cup of fresh Papaya, chopped

1 cup of Strawberries

Method:
Blend all the ingredients until smooth and creamy! Enjoy!

3.10 Mixed Berry, Spinach and Orange smoothie

Berries, spinach and orange are some of the top foods for good skin and glowing complexion. This is a great smoothie to have as a snack!

Serves – 2

Time – 5 Minutes

Ingredients:
2 handfuls of Baby Spinach

2 cups of Mixed Berries

1 Orange, peeled and sectioned

2 Tbsp. Hemp Meal

Method:
Blend all the ingredients until smooth. Serve immediately. Enjoy!

4.1 Cucumber and Coconut Smoothie

When you think of cucumber and coconut you think of water and hydration! This smoothie is amazingly hydrating and soothing.

Serves – 2

Time – 5 Minutes

Ingredients:

1 Cucumber, washed and peeled

2 cups of Coconut water

1 cup of fresh Coconut meat

A small knob of Ginger

½ cup Parsley

Mint leaves for garnish

Method:

Blend all the ingredients until creamy! Add extra honey for added sweetness.

4.2 Spicy Watermelon and Cantaloupe Smoothie

You will love the simplicity and delicious taste of this smoothie, perfect for hydrating yourself during the summer heat!

Serves – 2

Time – 5 Minutes

Ingredients:
2 cups of Watermelon, chopped

2 cups of Cantaloupe, chopped

A pinch of Cinnamon

A pinch of Nutmeg

Method:
Blend all the ingredients until smooth and creamy!

4.3 Strawberry, Spinach and Lemonade Smoothie

Delicious! This smoothie is a great combination of taste and health benefits. Every ingredient lends taste and abundant health benefits!

Serves – 2

Time – 5 Minutes

Ingredients:
1 cup of fresh Strawberries

2 handfuls of Baby Spinach

2 cups of Lemonade

A small knob of Ginger

A pinch of Sea Salt

Method:
Blend all the ingredients for 15-20 seconds. Serve immediately! Enjoy!

4.4 Spinach, Green Apple and Cucumber Smoothie

This smoothie is a vivid green smoothie that is extremely nutritious and hydrating. It is great for replenishing your body with water and all the healthy nutrients.

Serves – 2

Time – 5 Minutes

Ingredients:
2 Green Apples

1 Cucumber

2 handfuls of Baby Spinach

1 Tsp of Spirulina

A small knob of Ginger

A pinch of Sea Salt

Method:
Blend all the ingredients until smooth. Serve on ice cubes if you prefer. Enjoy!

4.5 Yoghurt and Papaya smoothie

This smoothie is both cooling and hydrating. The papaya contains papain which is a very useful enzyme to maintain good health. Yoghurt adds the protein and creamy texture to this refreshing smoothie!

Serves – 2

Time – 5 Minutes

Ingredients:
2 cups of fresh Papaya, cubed

2 cups of Vanilla Yoghurt

4-6 Dates, for sweetness

A pinch of Sea Salt

Method:
Blend all the ingredients in a blender until smooth and creamy. Enjoy!

4.6 Cucumber, Raspberry and Pineapple Smoothie

This smoothie is packed with amazing water content and nutrients essential for good health. It is a delicious recipe that will be loved by all.

Serves-2

Time-5 Minutes

Ingredients:

1 Cucumber, peeled and cut

1 cup of Raspberries (fresh/frozen)

2 cups of Pineapples, chopped

A small knob of Ginger

A pinch of Salt

Method:
Blend all the ingredients in a blender until smooth and creamy. Enjoy!

4.7 Blueberry, Watermelon and Tomato Medley

This smoothie is beautiful to look at and is a bounty of nutrition. The blueberry and watermelon are a great classical combination whereas the tomato adds a distinct savoury taste!

Serves – 2

Time – 5 Minutes

Ingredients:
1 cup of frozen Blueberries

2 cups of Watermelon, sliced

1 cup of Tomato, chopped

A small knob of Ginger

Few Mint leaves

Method:
Blend all the ingredients in the blender until smooth and creamy. Enjoy!

4.8 Summer Bonanza!

This smoothie is super delicious and lush. The combination of pineapple, watermelon and coconut is very tropical and is fantastic to quench your thirst and replenish your tired body!

Serves - 2

Time – 5 Minutes

Ingredients:
1 cup of Pineapple, chopped

1 cup of Watermelon, chopped

1 cup of Coconut water

1 cup of Fresh Coconut meat

Few sprigs of Mint

Blend all the ingredients into a blender until smooth and creamy! Enjoy

4.9 Strawberry-Grape and Coconut water Smoothie

This is a great smoothie, it almost tastes like dessert! Very fresh, hydrating and amazing to taste!

Serves – 2
Time – 5 Minutes

Ingredients:
1 cup of Strawberries, diced

1 cup of Black Grapes,

2 cups of Coconut Water

2 Tsp of Sunflower Seeds

Method:
Blend all the ingredients into a blender until smooth. Enjoy over ice!

4.10 Iceberg Lettuce, Star Fruit and Pear Smoothie

All the ingredients in this smoothie are high in water content! This smoothie is both thick and creamy and tart and sweet!

Serves – 2

Time – 5 Minutes

Ingredients:
A handful of Iceberg Lettuce

A handful of Baby Spinach

½ cup of Star fruit

2 Pears, cubed

A small knob of Ginger

Method:
Blend all the ingredients until smooth! Serve immediately!

5.1 Watermelon, Beetroot and Date Smoothie

Perfect snacks are both delicious and healthy! This smoothie is just that!

Serves – 2
Time – 5 Minutes

Ingredients:

2 ½ cups of Watermelon, cubed

½ a Beetroot

4-6 Dates

A small knob of Ginger

2 Tbsp. of Lemon juice

Method:
Blend all the ingredients until smooth. Serve over ice. Enjoy!

5.2 Spinach, Kiwi and Hemp Smoothie

Deliciously green this smoothie will definitely tickle your taste buds! The hemp seeds make this wonderful smoothie a healthy snack for you!

Serves – 2

Time – 5 Minutes

Ingredients:
2 handfuls of Baby Spinach

2 Kiwis, peeled and cut

1 Tbsp. Hemp Seeds

1 ½ cup of Lemonade

Method:
Blend all the ingredients in a blender and blend until smooth. Serve over ice if preferred. Enjoy!

5.3 Dragon Fruit, Spinach and Blueberry Smoothie

This smoothie is fruity but contains a healthy dose of the greens that are amazing for your health! This smoothie is great to have over ice, sure to make you swoon!

Serves – 2

Time – 5 Minutes

Ingredients:
1 cup of Dragon Fruit, cubed

2 handfuls of Baby Spinach

1 cup Blueberries

1 cup of Lemonade

A small knob of Ginger

Method:
Blend all the ingredients until smooth. Serve immediately. Enjoy!

5.4 Mango, Apricot and Kale Smoothie

This is an apricot twist to a classic yet delicious mango and kale smoothie!

Serves – 2

Time – 5 Minutes

Ingredients:
3 large leaves of Dinosaur Kale

2 cups of fresh Mango, cubed

½ cup of Apricots, chopped

2 Tbsp. of Lemon juice

1 Tbsp. whole Flaxseed

Method:
Blend all the ingredients until smooth and creamy. Enjoy!

5.5 Figs, Spinach and Strawberry Smoothie

Figs and spinach are both great to improve your overall health and contain a lot of iron, something you need in order to glow from with! Strawberry adds a berry twist to this smoothie!

Serves - 2

Time - 5 Minutes

Ingredients:

3 handfuls of Baby Spinach

2-3 fresh Figs, chopped

1 cup of Strawberry

2 tsp of Chia Seeds

Method
Blend all the ingredients until well combined and serve immediately. Enjoy!

5.6 Kale, Honey Dew and Date Smoothie

Honey dew is a sweet thirst quencher which works miracles for your skin and overall health! Kale and dates add more nutrients and body to this smoothie!

Serves – 2

Time – 5 Minutes

Ingredients:
2 cups of Honey Dew, cubed

2-3 large leaves of Dinosaur Kale

4-5 Dates

2 Tbsp. Lime Juice

Few sprigs of Mint

Method:
Blend all ingredients until smooth and well combined. Enjoy!

5.7 Avocado, Collard Greens and Figs Smoothie

This green smoothie is very easy to fall in love with. The creamy avocado and sweet figs add wonderful taste to the mildly bitter collards!

Serves – 2

Time – 5 Minutes

Ingredients:
1 cup of Collard Greens

1 ripe Avocado

2-3 fresh ripe Figs

1 Lemon, rind removed and sectioned

2 Tsp of Spirulina

Method:
Blend all the ingredients until smooth and creamy. Enjoy!

5.8 Blueberry, Orange and Vanilla Yoghurt Smoothie

Blueberry and orange are tangy, sweet and delicious. Though they are great on their own, but when combined with vanilla yoghurt it is much creamier and tasty!

Serves – 2

Time – 5 Minutes

Ingredients:
1 cup of Blueberries

2 Oranges, peeled and sectioned

2 cups of Vanilla yoghurt

2 Tbsp. Hemp seeds

2 Tbsp. Lemon juice

Method:
Blend all the ingredients until smooth and creamy. Enjoy!

5.9 Pineapple, Strawberry and Grape Fruit Smoothie

This smoothie should be officially renamed as the Vitamin C smoothie. Rich in vitamin C and bountiful of anti-oxidants, this makes for a great smoothie snack!

Serves – 2

Time – 5 Minutes

Ingredients:
2 cups of fresh Pineapple, cubed

1 cup of Strawberry

1 cup of Grape Fruit juice

1 cup of Lemonade

A small knob of Ginger

Method:
Blend all the ingredients until smooth and well combined. Enjoy!

5.10 Dragon Fruit, Carrot and Kale Smoothie with Cocoa

This smoothie is hearty and delicious to taste. The dragon fruit gives a unique sweet taste to the popular combination of carrot and kale!

Serves – 2

Time – 5 Minutes

Ingredients:
½ cup of Dragon Fruit

2 Carrots, peeled and cut

2-3 large leaves of Dinosaur Kale

2 cups of Lemonade

1 tsp Cocoa powder

A small knob of Ginger

1 Tbsp. whole Flaxseeds

Method:
Blend all the ingredients until smooth and creamy. Serve immediately. Enjoy!

6.1 Mango Vanilla Smoothie

This delicious Mango smoothie has great flavor with a sweet Vanilla twist! It is a creamy delight, thanks to the mango and avocado!

Serves – 2

Time – 5 Minutes

Ingredients:
½ cup Mango cubes

½ cup Ripe Avocado

½ Cup Vanilla Yoghurt

1 Tbsp. Lemon Juice

1 Tbsp. Maple Syrup

Ice Cubes (optional)

Method:
Blend all the ingredients in a blender until Smooth! Garnish with fresh mint leaves.

6.2 Blueberry and Coconut Surprise

This gorgeous looking smoothie is bursting with flavor and antioxidants and is a total delight to the senses! You will love the soothing and delectable taste of this smoothie!

Serves-2

Time- 5 minutes

Ingredients:

1 Cup Frozen or fresh Blueberries

1 Cup of Coconut Flesh

1 Cup of Coconut Milk

1 Tbsp Wild Honey

A pinch of Himalayan salt (optional)

Method:
Blend all the ingredients until smooth and creamy. Serve in a tall glass with few blueberries for garnish. Enjoy!

6.3. Vanilla Yoghurt and Raspberry Smoothie

This smoothie is a yummy way to lose weight without compromising tour taste buds! This is an excellent dessert to have!

Serves - 2
Time – 5 Minutes
Ingredients:
2 cups of Vanilla Flavored Yoghurt
1 cup of Frozen Raspberries
1 cup of Coconut water
1 Tbsp. Pomegranate Molasses
Method:
Blend all the ingredients until smooth and has a silky consistency. Serve in a glass and top it with few raspberries. Enjoy!

6.4 Omega 3 Rich Peach Smoothie

This smoothie is rich in Omega 3 fatty acids and is a healthy-nutritious way to loosing belly fat! Omega-3 fatty acids are essential for our well-being and health!

Serves - 2

Time – 5 Minutes

Ingredients:

2 cups Almond milk

2 cups Peaches, chopped, frozen

4 Tbsp. cold pressed Flaxseed Oil

2 Tsp Wild Honey (optional)

2 Tsp whole Flax seeds (optional)

Method:

Blend all the ingredients in a blender until smooth and delicious. Enjoy within 15 minutes for best results.

6.5 Apple and Coconut-Vanilla Smoothie

The sweet and tarty taste of apple combined with the aromatic vanilla is a real winner. And it is incredibly healthy too!

Serves – 2
Time – 10 Minutes
Ingredients:
2 cups Apples, sliced
2 cups cold Coconut milk
½ cup Coconut Flesh
1 Tsp vanilla extract
1 Tsp Cinnamon powder
Ice cubes (optional)
Method:
Blend all the ingredients and thick and creamy. Serve in a tall glass and eat with a spoon. Enjoy!

6.6 Pineapple and Spiced Pumpkin Smoothie

This smoothie is thick and luscious. The warm pie spice adds an earthy tone to this delicious nutrient rich smoothie!

Serves – 2

Time – 10 Minutes

Ingredients:

1 ½ cups of Cubed ripe Pineapples

1 ½ cups of Cubed Pumpkins

1 Tsp Pumpkin Pie Spice

1 ½ cups of Almond milk

2 Tsp Maple Syrup (optional, for more sweetness)

Method:

Blend all the ingredients until smooth and creamy. Serve in a tall glass and dig in with a spoon!

6.7 Strawberry and Pomegranate Smoothie

This gorgeous smoothie is super healthy and is loaded with disease fighting anti-oxidants! The luscious strawberries with almost garnet colored pomegranate seeds yield this amazing delight!

Serves – 2

Time – 10 Minutes

Ingredients:
1 ½ cups of strawberries diced frozen

1 cup pomegranate seeds

2 cups of low fat yoghurt/ skim milk

2 Tbsp. Cold pressed Flax seed oil

Method:
Blend all the ingredients in a blender until smooth and creamy! Enjoy as breakfast or a mid-day Snack!

6.8 Green Tea, Kale and Papaya Smoothie

This is a great smoothie for so many reasons! Powerful enzymes, nutrients and anti oxidants make it incredibly healthy, and the taste is delectable too!

Serves – 2

Time – 5 Minutes

Ingredients:
2 leaves of Dinosaur Kale

1 ½ cup of fresh Papaya, chopped

2 cups of strong Chinese Green Tea

A small knob of Ginger

A pinch of Sea Salt

Method:
Blend all the ingredients until smooth and creamy! Enjoy!

6.9 The Green Delight Smoothie

This smoothie is not like most green smoothies that are nutritious but horrible to taste. Meet the smoothie that is so tasty, you won't believe it's that healthy!

Serves – 2

Time – 10 Minutes

Ingredients:

1 medium cucumber, peeled and cubed

2 handfuls baby spinach

2 cups of pear, diced

1 Tsp of Himalayan/sea salt

Method:
Blend all the ingredients until smooth. This is a great hydrating and slimming smoothie, perfect for a post workout snack!

6.10 Papaya, Banana and Green apple Smoothie

This smoothie is a great snack option and is great for digestion as well! The papaya and banana add the creaminess while the green apple adds the much added sweet-tarty flavor to this delicious smoothie!

Serves – 2

Time – 5 Minutes

Ingredients:
1 cup of Papaya, cubed

1 banana, diced

1 green apple, chopped

1 cup coconut water

Ice cubes (optional)

Method:
Blend all the ingredients in a blender and serve on ice if you prefer. Enjoy!

7.1 Honeydew, Cucumber and Ginger Smoothie

Melons and cucumber are great for gut health as they contain a lot of water and ease the elimination process.

Serves – 2

Time – 5 Minutes

Ingredients:

1 Cucumber, peeled and cut

2 cups of Honey Dew, chopped

1 cup of Lemonade

A small knob of Ginger

Method:

Blend all the ingredients into a blender, until smooth. Enjoy!

7.2 Apple, Apple Cider Vinegar and Beetroot Smoothie

This smoothie is rich in pectin and nutrients that keep your gut healthy!

Serves – 2

Time - 5 Minutes

Ingredients:
2 Apples, cut

½ a medium Beetroot

2 Tbsp Apple Cider Vinegar

2 cups of Kefir

A small knob of Ginger

Method:
Blend all the ingredients until smooth. Serve immediately. Add honey for extra sweetness, if needed.

7.3 Banana, Avocado and Aloe Vera Smoothie

This creamy smoothie is a wonderful anecdote for your body to heal and work efficiently!

Serves – 2

Time – 5 Minutes

Ingredients:
1 ripe Banana

1 Avocado

2 cups of Lemonade

½ cup Aloe Vera juice

A small knob of Ginger

Few sprigs of Mint

Method:
Blend all the ingredients until smooth and creamy! Serve immediately.

7.4 Green Tea, Papaya and Spinach Smoothie

This smoothie that is rich with anti-oxidants and enzymes that are great for you!

Serves – 2

Time – 5 Minutes

Ingredients:
2 cups of strong Chinese Green Tea, cooled

1 cup of fresh ripe Papaya

2 handfuls of baby Spinach

A knob of Ginger

2 Tsp Lemon juice

2 Tbsp. whole Flaxseeds

1 Tbsp. Honey (optional)

Method:

Blend all the ingredients until smooth. Serve immediately!

7.5 Pineapple, Avocado and Parsley Smoothie

This creamy and fruity smoothie makes sure you get all the necessary enzymes and oils that are great for you!

Serves – 2

Time – 5 Minutes

Ingredients:
1 cup of fresh ripe Pineapple, chopped

½ an Avocado

A handful of Parsley

2 cups of Coconut water

½ Tsp of Probiotic powder

Method:
Blend all the ingredients until smooth and creamy! Serve it over ice if desired.

7.6 Super Smoothie with garlic and ACV

This is a smoothie which has a savory garlicky kick yet delicious to taste! There are hundreds of reasons why garlic and apple cider vinegar are good for! A must try!

Serves – 2

Time – 5 Minutes

Ingredients:

2 Apples, cubed

2 Carrots, peeled and cut

A clove of Garlic

2 Tbsp. Apple Cider Vinegar

Few sprigs of Mint

A small knob of Ginger

Method:
Blend all the ingredients until smooth and creamy! Serve immediately.

7.7 Kale, Almond Milk and Mixed Berry Smoothie

This is a berry take on a classic creamy green smoothie! It is a one you should definitely try!

Serves – 2

Time – 5 Minutes

Ingredients:

3-4 large leaves of Dinosaur Kale

2 cups of Mixed Berries, fresh or frozen

2 cups of Almond milk

1 Tbsp whole Flaxseeds

Method:
Blend all the ingredients until smooth and creamy! Enjoy!

7.8 Mango and Papaya Smoothie with Turmeric

A mango-papaya smoothie with a turmeric spice twist! Turmeric has great anti-inflammatory and anti-bacterial benefits making it perfect to maintain good gut health!

Serves – 2

Time – 5 Minutes

Ingredients:

2 cups of fresh Mango, chopped

1 cup of Papaya, chopped

1 Tsp of Turmeric powder

1 ½ cup of Coconut water

Method:
Blend all the ingredients until smooth and creamy. Serve chilled. Enjoy.

7.9 Cranberry and Creamy Coconut Smoothie

Cranberry is one of the berries that has been tried and tested by ancient doctors and conventional medicine alike for its amazing healing and restorative qualities!

Serves - 2

Time – 5 Minutes

Ingredients:
¾ cup of Cranberries

1 ripe Banana, peeled and cut

2 cups of tender Coconut meat

1 Tbsp whole Flaxseeds

1 Tbsp Maple syrup (optional)

Method:
Blend all the ingredients until smooth and creamy! Serve immediately!

7.10 Dragon Fruit-Avocado and Almond Milk Smoothie

This is one smoothie that you will fall in love with! Dragon fruit with its exotic taste and health benefits combines with creamy avocado and delicious almond milk makes this smoothie a real winner!

Serves – 2

Time – 5 Minutes

Ingredients:
½ cup of Dragon Fruit

1 Avocado

2 cups of Almond milk

A small knob of Ginger

1 Tbsp Lemon juice

1 Tbsp Honey (optional)

Method:
Blend all the ingredients until smooth and creamy! Serve immediately and enjoy!

8.1 Creamy Avocado and Cucumber Smoothie

This creamy smoothie is made from avocado, cucumber and coconut meat which all alkaline ingredients!

Serves – 2

Time – 5 Minutes

Ingredients:
1 ripe Avocado

1 Cucumber, peeled and cubed

1 cup of Coconut Meat

1 ½ cup of Coconut Water

A small knob of Ginger

1 Tbsp. Wild Honey

Blend all the ingredients into a blender and blend until smooth. Enjoy!

8.2 Peach, Spinach and Banana Smoothie

This smoothie is delicious and great for alkalizing your body. It contains healthy fruits and vegetables that have great alkalizing properties!

Serves – 2

Time – 5 Minutes

Ingredients:
1 ripe Banana

2 handfuls of Baby Spinach

2 Peaches, chopped

2 Tbsp. of Lemon juice

A pinch of Sea Salt

Method:
Blend all the ingredients in a blender until smooth. Serve immediately.

8.3 Pineapple, Spinach and Almond Milk Smoothie

Pineapple has great healing properties due to its enzyme bromelain which is a great digestive enzyme. Together with spinach and almond milk, it's a incredibly healthy smoothie!

Serves – 2

Time – 5 Minutes

Ingredients:
2 cups of ripe Pineapple, chopped

2 handfuls of Baby Spinach

2 cups of Almond Milk

1 Tbsp. of Chia seeds

Method:
Blend all the ingredients until smooth and creamy. Enjoy!

4. Kale, Banana and Spirulina Smoothie

Kale is one of the most nutrient dense vegetables on this planet. Spirulina is a superfood which is dense in nutrient value as well. When both these ingredients are blended with banana you get an amazingly alkalizing smoothie!

Serves – 2

Time – 5 Minutes

Ingredients:
3 large leaves of Dinosaur Kale leaves

1 ripe Banana

2 Tsp Spirulina powder

2 cups of Coconut milk

Method:

Blend all the ingredients in a blender and serve immediately!

8.5 Dandelion, Apple and Flaxseed Smoothie

This smoothie contains a dandelion greens which are very alkaline and when combined with apple that contains pectin and flaxseed which are rich in omega-3 fatty acids, you get a tasty and nutritious smoothie.

Serves – 2

Time – 5 Minutes

Ingredients:
1 cup of Dandelion Greens

1 cup of Baby Spinach

1 Apple, diced

2 Tbsp. whole Flaxseed

1 ripe Banana

Method:
Blend all the ingredients until smooth. Pour in a chilled glass and enjoy!

8.6 Carrot, Avocado and Ginger Smoothie

Carrot and avocado are a great combination that is nutrient rich and highly alkalizing. It provides the body valuable nutrition and this smoothie is a great way to get the best from these ingredients!

Serves – 2

Time – 5 Minutes

Ingredients:
2 Carrots, peeled and cut
1 ripe Avocado
2 cups of Lemonade
A small knob of Ginger
A pinch of Sea Salt

Method:
Blend all the ingredients into a blender and blend until smooth and creamy! Enjoy!

8.7 Romaine Lettuce, Pineapple and Pumpkin Seed Smoothie

This smoothie is a great way to have beneficial greens in your diet. Both romaine lettuce and pineapple are alkalizing and great to maintain optimum health!

Serves – 2

Time – 5 Minutes

Ingredients:
2 handfuls of Romaine Lettuce

2 cups of Pineapple

2 Tbsp. Pumpkin Seeds

1 cup of Coconut Milk

A small knob of Ginger

A pinch of Sea Salt

Method:
Blend all the ingredients

8.8 Minty Kale, Strawberry-Coconut Smoothie

This brilliant smoothie is superbly delicious and healthy all at once. All the ingredients in this smoothie impart amazing healing and alkaline properties.

Serves – 2

Time – 5 Minutes

Ingredients:
2-3 large leaves of Dinosaur Kale

1 cup of Strawberries

1 cup of Coconut Meat

½ cup of Mint Leaves

1 cup of Lemonade

A small knob of ginger

1 Tbsp of Agave Nectar

Method:
Blend all the ingredients until smooth and delicious! Enjoy!

8.9 Avocado, Baby Greens and Date Smoothie

This sweet and creamy green smoothie will revolutionize the way you look at green smoothies. Dates lend this green smoothie its unique sweetness while the avocado lends a creamy nutritious dimension.

Serves – 2

Time – 5 Minutes

Ingredients:
2 cups of Baby Greens

1 ripe Avocado

½ cup of Dates, pitted or seedless

2 cups of Coconut Water

Method:
Blend all the ingredients until smooth and creamy! Serve immediately!

8.10 Kale, Grapes and Cucumber Smoothie

Kale, grapes and cucumber are all very alkaline food ingredients. Blended together these ingredients produce a healthy and tasty smoothie that will be loved by all.

Serves - 2

Time – 5 minutes

Ingredients:
3 large leaves of Dinosaur Kale

2 cups of Black Grapes

1 Cucumber, peeled and cut

2 tsp of Spirulina

Method:
Blend all the ingredients until smooth and creamy! Serve immediately!

9.1 Pineapple and Ginger Smoothie

Simple and straightforward- this smoothie is amazing for you and has enormous health benefits with live enzymes and anti-inflammatory benefits!

Serves – 2

Time – 5 Minutes

Ingredients:
2 cups of ripe Pineapple, cubed

2 cups of Coconut Water

A small knob of Ginger

Method:

Blend all the ingredients in a blender until smooth and creamy. Enjoy over ice if preferred.

9.2 Sweet and Creamy Spinach Smoothie

This reviving smoothie will surely boost your metabolism. Celery, pear and banana give the humble spinach smoothie a sweet and savory twist!

Serves – 2

Time – 5 Minutes

Ingredients:
2 handfuls of Baby Spinach

2 stalks of Celery

1 ripe Banana

1 Pear

1 cup of Coconut Water

2 Tbsp. of Lemon juice

A small knob of Ginger

Method:
Blend all the ingredients until smooth. Serve immediately!

9.3 Papaya, Pineapple and Carrot Smoothie

Start your day with this energetic and zingy smoothie made with fruits and veggies with live enzymes that help you burn fat!

Serves – 2

Time – 5 Minutes

Ingredients:

2 cups of ripe Papaya, cubed

1 cup of ripe Pineapple, cubed

1 Carrot, peeled and cut

1 Lemon, rind removed

A small knob of Ginger

Method:

Blend all the ingredients in a blender and blend until well combined. Serve over ice. Enjoy!

-

9.4 Pumpkin, Pear and Ginger Smoothie

This glorious smoothie will drive your metabolism into kick-drive! The ginger in this smoothie aids fat-loss!

Serves – 2

Time – 5 Minutes

Ingredients:

2 cups of Pumpkin, cubed

1 Pear

2 cups of Coconut Milk

A knob of Ginger

Method:
Blend all the ingredients in a blender and blend until smooth and creamy. Enjoy!

9.5 Kale, Yoghurt and Banana Smoothie

Kale your way to improve your metabolism! A healthy smoothie with kale helps increase your metabolism and lose fat!

Serves – 2

Time – 5 Minutes

Ingredients:
3-4 large leaves of Dinosaur Kale

1 ripe Banana

2 cups of Plain Yoghurt

1 Tbsp. of Agave Nectar

1 Tbsp. of Sunflower Seeds

Method:
Blend all the ingredients until smooth and well combined. Enjoy!

9.6 Beetroot, Cucumber and Green Apple Smoothie

Beetroot, cucumber and green apple- all 3 of them help improve your metabolism and keep you healthy and hydrated!

Serves - 2

Time – 5 Minutes

Ingredients:
1 Cucumber, peeled and cut

½ a Beetroot

2 Green Apples, cubed

1 inch of Ginger

1 Tbsp. of whole Flaxseeds

Method:
Blend all the ingredients until smooth. Serve over ice if preferred. Enjoy!

9.7 Broccoli, Strawberry and Almond Milk Smoothie

Vitamin B is essential to turn carbohydrates, fats and proteins into energy- which is found abundantly in broccoli! Alerting your body to work faster and more efficiently is as simple as making sure you have your dose of broccoli!

Serves – 2

Time – 5 Minutes

Ingredients:
1 ½ cup of Broccoli florets

1 cup of Strawberries

1 ½ Almond milk

1 Tbsp. of Chia seeds

Method:
Blend all the ingredients in a blender until smooth and creamy. Enjoy!

-

9.8 Avocado, Spinach and Green Grapes Smoothie

This smoothie should be re-names green revolution! Not only for it's bright vivid green color but also for its amazing reviving and restorative qualities that help boost your metabolism!

Serves – 2

Time – 5 Minutes

Ingredients:
2 handfuls of Baby Spinach

1 ripe Avocado

2 cups of Green Grapes

½ cup of Walnuts

1 Tsp of Spirulina

A small knob of Ginger

1 Tbsp. of Lime Juice

Method:
Blend all the ingredients in a blender until smooth. Serve immediately.

9.9 Carrot, Beetroot and Apple Smoothie

This combination is often regarded as the Miracle blend by many people! The reason it is called so is because it has miraculous health benefits. With the ginger thrown in, it makes for a more powerful metabolic booster!

Serves – 2

Time – 5 Minutes

Ingredients:
2 Carrots, peeled and cut

2 Apples, cubed

½ a Beetroot

A small knob of Ginger

2 Tbsp. Lemon Juice

Method:
Blend all the ingredients until smooth. Serve immediately.

10. Kale and Grapefruit Smoothie

Kale and grapefruit are both great metabolism boosters in themselves! Combined with fresh lime juice or lemonade, what you get is a killer combination!

Serves – 2

Time – 5 Minutes

Ingredients:
3-4 large leaves of Dinosaur Kale

1 Grapefruit, peeled and cubed

½ cup of Cashews

2 cups of Coconut milk

2 Tsp of Spirulina

1 Tbsp. Sunflower seeds

1 Tbsp. of Agave Nectar (optional)

Method:
Blend all the ingredients until smooth and creamy. Serve immediately!

10.1 Raspberry - Pomegranate Smoothie

This smoothie is super-packed with anti-oxidants as it contains raspberries and pomegranate seeds. It is a lush creamy smoothie that will truly satisfy your food cravings!

Serves – 2

Time – 5 Minutes

Ingredients:
1 cup Raspberry

1 cup Pomegranate seeds

1 cup Greek yoghurt

1 cup Coconut water

1 ripe Banana

Method:
Blend these ingredients until smoothie is thick and creamy. The antioxidants in this smoothie help boost your immunity and keep you healthy.

10.2 Almond and Mixed Berry smoothie

This superb tasting smoothie is both healthy and highly gratifying! Since it is naturally sweet and lush, you can even have it as dessert!

Serves – 2

Time – 5 Minutes

Ingredients:
2 cups Almond milk

6-7 Almonds

1 1/2 cup Mixed frozen Berries

1 tsp of wild honey (optional)

Method:
Blend all these ingredients until smooth and serve immediately. The vitamins and minerals present in the almonds and berries make this smoothie a delicious and nutritious way of boosting your immunity.

10.3 Banana and Apple-Ginger Smoothie

Let this simple smoothie recipe not trick you! The ingredients are very simple but the taste is very compound and robust! This smoothie is great to be had as breakfast!

Serves – 2

Time – 10 Minutes

Ingredients:

2 ripe Bananas

2 Apples chopped

A small knob of Ginger

2 serving of Protein powder

1 cup of low fat Milk

Method:
Blend all these ingredients until smooth and creamy. This is an amazing and super healthy way to increase your body immunity.

10.4 Green tea, Berry and Papaya Smoothie

This smoothie spells healthy! The green tea, berries and papaya are great for your immunity! It is instantly energizing and super delicious! You will love it!

Serves – 2

Time – 10 Minutes

Ingredients:
2 cups of strong Green tea, cooled

2 cups of Mixed frozen Berries

1 cup chopped ripe Papaya

2 serving of Whey Protein powder

Method:
Blend the banana and berries for 10 seconds. Add the remaining ingredients and blend until smooth and creamy. Serve immediately and enjoy!

10.5 Pineapple and Pistachio Yoghurt Smoothie

If you like pineapples and pistachios, you will love this delicious smoothie recipe. It is light, fresh and smells wonderful. The enzymes from the pineapple and the nutrients from the pistachios make this smoothie refreshingly nutritious!

Serves – 2

Time – 5 Minutes

Ingredients:
2 cups chopped pineapple

½ cup of shelled dry roasted pistachios

2 cup low fat yoghurt

A small knob of ginger

2 servings of whey protein

1 tsp of wild honey (optional)

Method:
Blend all the ingredients in the blender until smooth. This smoothie is like a meal in itself. Enjoy!

10.6 Spinach, Kiwi and Pear Smoothie

This green smoothie will definitely be loved by all. Energy Boosting and instantly refreshing, this nutrient packed smoothie will help boost your immunity!

Serves – 2

Time – 10 Minutes

Ingredients:

4 Kiwis skinned

1 handful of Baby Spinach

2 Pears diced

2 tsp of Spirulina

1 cup Coconut Water

A small piece of Ginger

Method:
Blend all the ingredients in the blender until smooth and creamy. This smoothie is rich in Vitamin C and antioxidants and can be enjoyed as a mid-day snack!

www.ingramcontent.com/pod-product-compliance
Lightning Source LLC
Chambersburg PA
CBHW071438070526
44578CB00001B/132